HOW TO BE FREE

ANCIENT WISDOM FOR MODERN READERS

Ancient Wisdom for Modern Readers presents the timeless
and timely ideas of classical thinkers in lively new translations. Enlightening
and entertaining, these books make the practical wisdom of the ancient
world accessible for modern life.

■ ■ ■ ■

HOW TO BE FREE

■　■　■　■　■

An Ancient Guide to the Stoic Life

Epictetus

Encheiridion and Selections
from *Discourses*

*Translated and with an introduction
by A. A. Long*

PRINCETON UNIVERSITY PRESS

PRINCETON AND OXFORD

Published by Princeton University Press
41 William Street, Princeton, New Jersey 08540
6 Oxford Street, Woodstock, Oxfordshire OX20 1TR

press.princeton.edu

LCCN 2018935439
ISBN 978-0-691-17771-7

British Library Cataloging-in-Publication Data is available

Editorial: Rob Tempio and Matt Rohal
Production Editorial: Sara Lerner
Text and Jacket Design: Pamela Schnitter
Jacket Credit: Statue of unidentified Roman philosopher,
possibly the Stoic Euphrates. Heraklion Museum, Crete
Production: Erin Suydam
Publicity: Jodi Price
Copyeditor: Jay Boggis

This book has been composed in Stempel Garamond

Printed on acid-free paper. ∞

Printed in the United States of America

3 5 7 9 10 8 6 4 2

FOR DAVID

CONTENTS

INTRODUCTION

How to be free!? Is it a question or an exclamation, a political manifesto or a longing to go native, an aspiration for autonomy or the route to emancipation from bondage? This book presents an ancient Greek philosopher's take on freedom—freedom construed as living in agreement with nature, owning and ruling oneself, becoming a world citizen, desiring always and only what you are assured of getting—and much more. Epictetus (c. AD 55–135), our author and guide to the Stoic life, was born a slave (his Greek name means "acquired"), and entered service as a slave in the household of Epaphroditus, a power broker in Nero's Rome, and himself a freedman. By the time Epictetus publicly delivered his thoughts on freedom, he had enjoyed many years of manumission, but the experience of slavery left its mark on his philosophy through and through. The first lesson of the *Encheiridion*, his handbook guide to Stoicism, insists that everything that is truly our own doing is *naturally free, unimpeded, and unconstrained.*

Freedom, according to this notion, is neither legal status nor opportunity to move around at liberty. It is the mental orientation of persons who are impervious to frustration or disappointment because their wants and decisions depend on themselves and involve nothing that they cannot deliver to themselves. The Emperor Marcus Aurelius (reigned AD 161–180) took the point and reflected on it in his Stoic *Meditations*. And the novelist, Tom Wolfe, followed suit when, in his 1998 novel *A Man in Full*, he imagines his young hero escaping from both a literal and a metaphorical prison after reading and digesting the *Discourses* of Epictetus.

The chief constraint on personal freedom in ancient Greece and Rome was what Epictetus knew at first hand, the social practice and indignity of slavery. It was slavery, the condition of being literally owned and made to serve at another's behest that gave ancient freedom its intensely positive value and emotional charge. Slaves' bodily movements during their waking lives were strictly constrained by their masters' wishes and by the menial functions they were required to perform. But slaves, like everyone else, had minds, and minds as well as bodies are subject to freedom and constraint. You can be externally free and internally a slave, controlled by psychological masters in the form of disabling desires and passions and cravings. Conversely, you could be outwardly obstructed or even in literal bondage but internally free from frustration and disharmony, so free in fact that you found yourself in charge of your own well-being, lacking little or nothing that you could not provide for yourself. The latter, in essence, is the freedom that Epictetus, the ancient Stoic philosopher, made the central theme of his teaching.

Epictetus in His Time and Place

In the early years of the second century of our era, this ex-slave established a school for young men in the northwestern Greek city of Nicopolis, which had become a fashionable metropolitan center. One of his students was a brilliant youth called Arrian. Lucius Flavianus Arrianus, to give him his full name, was so impressed by his teacher's message that he produced eight books of *Discourses* from the lectures on Stoicism he had heard Epictetus deliver, writing them out in more or less verbatim form; and he also drafted the summary of them that we know as the *Encheiridion*, or handbook. The work you are presently reading, "How to Be Free," contains my translations of the *Encheiridion* and of nine excerpts from the four surviving books of *Discourses*. Arrian went on to have an illustrious career in Roman administration, and he published many other books including a history of Alexander the Great. We don't know how he managed to reproduce the actual words of Epictetus, but the text that has come down to us, written in *koinē*, the colloquial Greek also used in the New Testament, is clearly the voice of his teacher and not merely Arrian's adaptation of the way the philosopher spoke.

As a guide to the Stoic life, Epictetus's philosophy, especially in the *Encheiridion* format, has been popular ever since the text was first edited and printed in the sixteenth century. Translated and retranslated into numerous languages, his words strike home because they focus so sharply and memorably on situations that are the common lot of people at every time and place. The emotions to which he propounds remedy—fear, anxiety, envy, anger, resentment, grief—are everyone's experience, whether you live in Imperial Rome or modern America. To that extent Epictetus needs no introduction. Yet, while many of the scenarios he pictures are familiar place-fillers for our own experience, they also include his distinctive milieu and the mores of his distant time.

We find ourselves in a world that includes slaves (*Encheiridion* 12, 14, 26), public baths (ibid. 4, 45), games in the arena (ibid. 29, 33), and professional fortune tellers (ibid. 32). A hazard that Epictetus himself had experienced is exile (ibid. 21). Imperial Rome and its provinces were managed by a highly regimented and competitive system of offices and office holders (ibid. 19, 24). Jockeying for position was endemic, and it included looking for patrons, attending banquets, and seeking to impress influential figures (ibid, 19, 24, 25, 33). Epictetus dwells on the value of maintaining one's independence, which reminds us that his young students, like Arrian his recorder, were on the threshold of making their careers in the Imperial army or civil service. It was a male-dominated culture, as he indicates with his remarks about women and female roles (ibid. 40), but the *Encheiridion* in general has no obvious gender orientation, and it is completely free from machismo. The "you" and "we" Epictetus addresses could be any of us with minimal need to register cultural difference.

The Roman world of his lifetime was an absolute autocracy, headed by the emperor or Caesar. Epictetus rarely touches on politics, mentioning Caesar only once in this book's material (*Discourses* 3) and omitting all allusion to historical events. In the complete *Discourses* (e.g., 1.2) he does occasionally refer to historical figures who resisted imperial demands, but he stays completely silent concerning the emperors who ruled at the time of his teaching in Greece. Though freedom had been an important Stoic notion from the beginning, it owes its special importance in Epictetus not only because of his early life as a slave but also because the people he was addressing had no prospects of enjoying political autonomy.

Stoicism and Freedom

Stoic philosophy had originated in Greece at the end of the fourth century BC. Its founding fathers were eastern Mediterranean immigrants to Athens, which was no longer a vibrant democracy, as the city had been at the time of Socrates, but a client state of the kingdom of Macedonia. Loss of political autonomy was reflected in philosophy at Athens by an inward turn in the focus of ethics. Neither Stoicism nor Epicureanism, the other leading Hellenistic school, engaged strongly in political theory, as their predecessors Plato and Aristotle had done. The main focus of the younger philosophers' societal attention was not politics and legislation but personal well-being and self-improvement. This inward turn is strikingly illustrated by the way Stoic thought from its beginning treated freedom and slavery as primarily ethical and psychological denominators rather than marks of social status. According to Zeno, the original head of the Stoic school, freedom is the exclusive prerogative of those who are wise, while inferior persons, who comprise the majority of people, are not only fools but also slaves.

A first reaction to this claim could include shock at its intellectual elitism and its insensitivity to the plight of persons unfortunate enough to be literally enslaved. But now consider how radically Zeno's claim, in a slave-based economy, challenges the evaluation of persons in terms of the conventional servitude/freedom dichotomy. If wisdom is the true criterion of freedom, the principal burden of slavery shifts from the outer to the inner, from the physical to the mental, and philosophy not manumission becomes the source of liberty. You are enslaved, according to this uncompromising doctrine, if you set your heart on anything that is liable to impediment, whether because your body lets you down, or passions and emotions have you in their thrall, or you attach your well-being to things that depend on others—people, property, popularity, or simply luck.

In his celebrated essay "Two Concepts of Liberty," Isaiah Berlin distinguished between the "negative" notion of freedom *from* coercion (not being interfered with by others) and the "positive" notion of freedom *to be* or *to live* as one chooses (self-mastery or self-determination). For Epictetus these two notions come together so closely that they entail one another, as we can see in the following passage:

> Our master is anyone who has the power to implement or prevent the things that we want or don't want. Whoever wants to be free, therefore, should wish for nothing or avoid nothing that is up to other people. Failing that, one is bound to be a slave. (*Encheiridion* 14)

We could rewrite the second sentence along the lines: "Whoever wants to be free from coercion should restrict their wishes and aversions to things over which they have complete control."

How can we be sure that such choice is good for us and good for those whose company we share? Why be self-reliant rather than follow the ten commandments or some other set of time-honored principles? How can we know what to choose? The answer to these questions brings us back to Zeno's "wisdom" as the essence of freedom. His Greek word *sophia,* in its ordinary usage, can cover any kind of expertise, ranging from practical craftsmanship like carpentry to abstract knowledge such as geometry. In all cases, *sophia* signifies successful practice of a skill, and the skill that concerned Zeno and subsequent Stoic philosophers is the art of life. We can gloss this art as knowing how to live in harmony, harmony with our human nature and harmony with our social and physical environment. To achieve or try to achieve that understanding is the task of reason, and reason, according to Stoicism, is what makes human beings distinctive among animals (*Discourses* 7, 8).

Epictetus as Stoic Teacher

The texts of Epictetus that you will read here elaborate on these doctrines and explore their implications as guidance for everyday life. His contexts cover an enormous range of situations, ranging from mundane circumstances of family and professional life to challenging situations such as illness, poverty, and death. Epictetus does not distinguish sharply between morals and manners (see *Encheiridion* 33). Everything we are called on to do and think about is germane to his principal question: is this something that is up to me to decide and get started on, or should I accept it calmly and dispassionately as a situation that was brought about by things that are outside my control? A moment's reflection will show that the either/or question covers just about every imaginable situation. Someone is rude to you: that happening is outside your control, but you have complete freedom in how you respond to it. Accidents happen, a loved one dies, you don't get the job you applied for, you fall ill. None of this was your doing or responsibility, but in each case you are presented with something else that you can do, namely, treat the situation as an opportunity for exercising your own agency and assessment as distinct from taking yourself to be a victim of forces outside yourself, or as badly done to, or as singularly unfortunate.

Epictetus's message of freedom, when reduced to succinct modern terms, might seem to fit such homely advice as "Get real," "Grow up," "Show what you are made of," "Let it go," "Mind your own business." You can find more or less exact equivalents to these slogans in some of this book's translated materials. Their familiarity has much to do with the way ancient Stoicism has influenced Western thought and education since the time when Epictetus, Seneca, and Marcus Aurelius were first assimilated into European and American culture. It was these authors who gave rise to the modern sense of "philosophy" and "philosophical" as an outlook of serenity, calm, or resignation in the face of difficulties. These attitudes are not in vogue today because they don't fit the fashion for authenticity, expectation, display of feeling, and self-assertion. But in practice, as modern Stoic practitioners have found, they are timelessly relevant, and particularly applicable to our hectic world of social media, sound bites, validation, outrage, attention-seeking, and self-imposed anxiety.

"Get real" and so forth, as we use these watchwords today, have lost touch with their ancient Stoic underpinnings. As employed by Epictetus, they are advice on how persons can best organize their lives according to the

Stoic understanding of nature, psychology, and human values. Although Epictetus's voice is homely and informal, he was not himself a sloganeer. He was a popularizing presenter of an elaborate philosophical system, which relied, as any genuine philosophy must rely, on rigorous argument, internal coherence, and empirical justification.

One of his key words is nature (Greek *physis*). This term covers three interrelated areas: (1) the structure and contents of the physical world, hence the scope of our word "physics"; (2) human nature in respect to our mental faculties, aptitudes, and potentialities; and (3) the values that accord or fail to accord with human excellence and a flourishing life. As background to reading the *Encheiridion* and my selection of passages from the *Discourses*, here is a short review of these three areas of nature in Stoicism and of the way Epictetus uses them.

INTRODUCTION

Living in Harmony with Nature

1 *External Nature*: Epictetus follows his Stoic authorities in treating the physical world as an entirely determinate structure of causes and effects. Nothing happens purely by chance or for no reason; and so Stoics find it absurd to complain about natural events that were bound to occur. All phenomena are providentially caused by a rational agent (the Stoic divinity) that is immanent throughout everything, animate and inanimate (*Encheiridion* 31, *Discourses* 1), "the divine law by which all events are regulated" (Seneca, *Moral Letter* 76.23). Events conform to the divine law even when, from a purely human perspective, things may appear random or upsetting to conventional notions of benefit and harm. Epictetus presupposes a strict division between happenings attributable to nature

in this external sense, and human agency or will. This internal part of nature is the part that God, as a Stoic would say, has assigned to us as our opportunity and responsibility (*Discourses* 6 and 8). Nothing attributable to external nature is bad or capable of being different from the way it is (*Encheiridion* 27). As human beings, we can try to understand external nature and conform to it intelligently in our actions and attitudes, or we can resist it and be forcibly confronted with situations we are powerless to resist because of their natural causality (*Encheiridion* 53). The latter course is irrational, frustrating, and pointless—all that a Stoic seeks to avoid.

2 *Human nature*: In the first section of the *Encheiridion*, Epictetus lays out the psychological resources that enable mature persons to live freely within nature as defined in the previous paragraph. He uses the language of

freedom to mark off the mind from everything else that we ordinarily take to be basic
parts of our selves, including even our bodies and our acquired identities or standing in
the world. This extreme parsimony serves
him as the means to treat the mind as the one
and only domain in which people can, if they
so dispose themselves, be absolutely and unconditionally free, sovereign, and unimpeded.
Mind, he claims—taking mind to include
judgment, motivation, and volition—is entirely "up to us"; indeed it *is* us, if we focus on
our powers of self-determination and do not
allow things the world serves up to control
our desires and aversions (*Encheiridion* 2).

Epictetus has various ways of character-
izing the excellent life of a free human being. One of these expressions is the formula
"keeping one's will in harmony with nature"
(*Encheiridion* 4). The word I translate by

"will" (Greek *prohairesis*) can also be rendered by decision or choice. The Greek term covers both a person's general character and also the particular application of a choice and decision. Earlier Stoics called it the psychological faculty of "assent." You achieve harmony with nature and freedom by focusing your mind or will or assent on the things that you can control (desires, judgments, motivations) and accommodating yourself to the rest with the help of reason and understanding external nature.

Another favorite formula draws on the Stoic concept of impressions or appearances (Greek *phantasiai*). These are not simply thoughts due to imagination, as our derived word fantasies would suggest, but everything that comes into our minds all the time, whether we experience things that impinge on us through our senses, or thoughts that we deliberately evoke or ideas that simply arise involuntarily (*Encheiridion* 1, *Discourses* 7). Impressions can be clear or fuzzy, true or false, as simple as the sight of one's dog, as fictional as Superman, and as complex as the thought of a black hole. The range of impressions is unlimited, but what chiefly interest Epictetus are the kinds of mental events that challenge autonomy and tranquility because they are colored by strong feelings that can lead us astray. Everyone is affected from time to time by such impressions, and those experiences, taken just by themselves, are often spontaneous and outside our immediate control—a sexual fantasy, a panic attack, a worry about one's health or one's family, anxiety over the state of the world, and so on. What Epictetus insists we should do, in order to live as effectively as possible, is confront our impressions, especially those that disturb us, and accustom ourselves to manage them, interpret them, understand their occurrence, and thus bring them, or at least our response to them, under the control of our will and faculty of assent (*Discourses* 7, 9).

3 *Values*. Cardinal to these ideas about external nature and human nature is the Stoics' radical classification of values. To understand this feature of their philosophy, the following diagram will be of help.

Goods	Bads	Indifferents
Essentially beneficial	Essentially harmful	Neither essentially beneficial nor harmful
up to us	up to us	not up to us
virtue, wisdom, happiness	faultiness, folly, unhappiness	e.g., poverty, wealth
mind dependent	mind dependent	not mind dependent
harmony with nature	disharmony with nature	

The key to this classification of values is the notion that goodness and badness are entirely properties of people's minds, characters and actions—not properties of external nature or external events (*Encheiridion* 6, 19, 31). This doctrine restricts goodness and badness to the benefit or harm we do to ourselves by choosing and deciding to act and react as we do. Good and bad retain their basic sense of "beneficial" and "harmful" respectively, but Stoic philosophy confines the scope of benefit (goodness) and harm (badness) according to the criteria summarized in the diagram.

To qualify as good or bad, the only things that strictly count are essentially beneficial on the one hand and essentially harmful on the other hand. A good thing, for instance wisdom, is always and unconditionally beneficial to the wise person. Being beneficial is essential to wisdom, and by the same token folly is essentially harmful. Everything else falls into the category of indifferent things (Greek *adiaphora*, *Encheiridion* 32), meaning things that are neither essentially good/beneficial nor essentially bad/harmful. Many things count as indifferent because it would make no sense to value them positively or negatively, such as the number of hairs on one's head or choosing between this pea and that one. But the Stoics extend indifference to a great many things that people *naturally* do care about such as health and wealth, and they also extend indifference to things that people *naturally* dislike, such as illness and poverty.

In withholding goodness and badness from such things the Stoics initiated a huge and unending controversy, but they knew what they were doing, and no Stoic philosopher expressed that more trenchantly than Epictetus did (*Encheiridion* 6, 19, 24, 25, 29, 31, 32). Their linguistic and conceptual reform—for that is what it amounts to—asks us to face the following questions: (1) Are such conventional goods as health and wealth always and essentially beneficial to us? (2) Are they necessary to happiness? (3) Are they up to us? (4) Are they mind dependent? And (5) Are they harmonious with our rational nature? If unequivocal answers to all these questions are negative, as the Stoics concluded, we cannot be assured of happiness if we make it conditional on getting such things or on avoiding their opposites. Moreover, by making happiness conditional on circumstance, we surrender autonomy and equanimity, and put ourselves at risk of failure and disappointment. Conversely, by restricting goodness and benefit to the mind dependent qualities of virtue and wisdom, we can secure the happiness that accords with our nature as rational beings; and we can adapt ourselves effectively to external nature and whatever else is outside our own control.

When expressed in these stark terms, the Stoic doctrine will likely strike those who encounter it for the first time as impractical and inattentive to normal human aspirations. But there is much more to it than I have yet indicated. The Stoics agree, first of all, that we naturally prefer to be healthy and prosperous and that our natural attitude to the opposites of these conditions is negative. They agree, secondly, that we could not live a rational and harmonious life if we ignored these natural inclinations and disinclinations. However, natural preferences and dislikes need to be sharply distinguished from "desires" and "aversions," in which we *fully* commit our will and vest our expectations of happiness (*Encheiridion* 2). When we desire something or are averse to it, we typically treat the thing in question as a really big deal. Epictetus recommends us, then, not to "desire" health and premise our happiness on securing it, but accept it gratefully if it comes our way.

The crux of the issue then turns on the question of what is necessary and sufficient for happiness. As the Stoics see it, you *can* flourish in adverse situations and you *can* fail to live well in favorable ones. What makes for a successful human life, on this outlook, is fulfillment of one's nature as the rational animal that is one's birthright and goal (*Discourses* 8 and 9). In that endeavor what matters are not the gifts of fortune, obtaining natural preferences, and avoiding naturally dislikable things, but "making reason our decisive principle in everything" (*Encheiridion* 51), whether we encounter adversity or prosperity.

Readers must decide whether and to what extent they endorse this classification of values. In my opinion, the Stoics performed a great service in sharply distinguishing the category of mental benefits and harms (things "up to us," as Epictetus calls them) from the value of things whose causes are external to our individual intentions and responsibilities. The sharpness of the distinction highlights the ethical importance of recognizing the benefits and harms for which we are directly answerable by our intentions and emotional responses. Open to obvious challenge, though, are the presumptions that external events can be successfully insulated from the conditions for happiness and brought under the direct control of our will and desires. Isn't it natural and only human to think that happiness is heavily dependent on external circumstances? Is the Stoic way of life accessible to the ordinary fallible person that most of us are?

Epictetus can come across as heavy-handed and severe. But his purpose, as a teacher, was to show his students how to make *progress* (*Encheiridion* 12, 13, 48, 51) towards the Stoic goal and not settle for just being ordinary. He was well aware that acting consistently on the system of values I have outlined would be a counsel of perfection and even beyond himself. His focus is not on heroic achievement but approximating to it, trying it out on situations that typically trouble people and undermine their performance in everyday life. You don't have to endorse Stoic determinism and providential theology as the precondition for studying his regimen. However, his reverential stance toward divinity (*Encheiridion* 31, *Discourses* 7) fits our time and place completely if we interpret it as sensitivity to the blessings of the ecosystem. I strongly encourage readers to identify the salient features of these theories in Epictetus's deployment of them, and to aid in that identification I have appended a selection of references in this review of his philosophy of nature.

Freedom and Ethics

The Stoics' theory of goodness and badness puts them in the camp of philosophers who think that the proper objects of *moral* judgment are a person's will and intention as distinct from their actions' consequences. Yet the principal aim of the theory, as Epictetus presents it in the *Encheiridion*, appears to be the agent's own happiness and tranquility rather than that of other people. Such self-centeredness seems at odds with any deep interest in the needs of other human beings. In which case, do the *Encheiridion* and *Discourses* offer us a guide to the moral life, taking that notion to include the good of others as well as oneself, or acting entirely for their sake?

This is a question to which Epictetus has a remarkably effective response if you agree with him that "It is every creature's nature . . . to shun things that look harmful or cause harm, and to like the look of things that are beneficial or bring benefit . . . and that wherever people's interest lies, that's also the site of their reverence" (*Encheiridion* 31). Ethics according to this Stoic viewpoint starts from and must accommodate our basic human interest in our own individual benefit or good. We do not start from instincts of altruism. To make room, then, for the good of others, Epictetus needs to show that his message of mental freedom is not a solipsistic benefit but socially advantageous and consonant with living in harmony with human nature construed quite broadly.

As individuals, we benefit hugely from not being troubled by emotions like envy, jealousy, fear, and anger, and by having the corresponding virtues of patience and self-control (*Encheiridion* 10). Tranquility is an obvious good to the tranquil, but its benefits redound no less to our families, friends, and associates because negative emotions often motivate aggressive and hurtful behavior. In contemporary life "ethics" typically enters conversation in contexts where norms of conduct are *violated*, whether in business or sexual behavior or disturbances of the peace. Epictetus's freedom regimen satisfies the moral imperative to do no harm.

How is it with positive moral imperatives, not just refraining from harm but deliberately treating others with care and consideration? Can our interest in freedom and tranquility motivate us to be friendly and philanthropic? Stoic philosophers had traditionally argued that our instincts for self-preservation are combined with powerful social instincts, starting with family life and extending to local community and beyond. Epictetus does not address this doctrine explicitly in this book's material, but his endorsement of it is evident in numerous passages. He presupposes interest in supporting friends and country on condition that one maintains an honorable character in so acting (*Encheirion* 24, 32). He has much to say about appropriate "role-play" in family relationships, with emphasis on what is incumbent on oneself as distinct from what one can expect in return (*Encheiridion* 17, 24,

30, 32, 43). Here too his focus on freedom from disabling emotions comes forcefully into play, with the deadly quarrel between the sons of Oedipus, competing for the throne, being one of his most telling counter-examples (*Encheiridion* 31, *Discourses* 5).

His *memento mori* warnings concerning wife and children touch a bleak note (*Encheiridion* 3, 7, 11, 14)—until we reflect on the prevalence of infant mortality and premature death in his time. Rather than insensitivity, they betoken the strongest possible recommendation to care for loved ones as long as we are permitted to have them. The emotional freedom at the heart of his message has enormous ethical import in the space it provides for *us* and what *we can* do. Seneca, writing at the time of Nero, had said it memorably: "Freedom is the prize we are working for: not being a slave to anything—not to compulsion, not to chance events—making fortune meet us on a level playing field" (*Moral Letter* 51.9).

A Free Will?

"Will," my translation of Epictetus's key term *prohairesis*, can also be translated by "choice" or "decision," as I have said before. These things are "naturally free," he says, because they are "up to us" (*Encheiridion* 1); so it follows at once that Epictetus had some notion of a free will. Does it also follow that he believed in "the freedom of the will"? That expression is notoriously vague and obscure. It is sometimes taken to imply that one and the same person in the same situation *could have* chosen to act differently from how she does decide, giving her the option of a genuinely alternative future. We can call this notion indeterminist freedom.

That is not at all what Epictetus had in mind. His passionate advocacy of autonomy (e.g.,

Discourses 9) can give the impression that there are no limits to the mental scope of freedom, but this is hyperbole. Like his Stoic predecessors, Epictetus accepted "fate" (*Encheiridion* 53), meaning that nothing happens, including our own actions, without a predetermined cause. From the god's-eye perspective, the story of everyone's life is already fixed and settled, including the specific choices and decisions people will make. What interests Epictetus is not the history and opportunity of our decision making (whether you or I could have become different persons from how we turned out) but what we aim for with the choices and wishes that we actually make, and how we exercise our power of "assent" (*Discourses* 4, 6). "Whoever wants to be free should wish for nothing or avoid nothing that is up to other people" (*Encheiridion* 14).

Most of us of course are much more prodigal in our aspirations; we blithely risk subjection to fortune and to unachievable goals. In that way, according to Epictetus, people regularly forfeit the free will that is their natural and best potentiality. Freedom of will, on this construal—wishing for nothing that is not up to oneself—is not the general human condition, but an arduous philosophical achievement. It consists of a state of mind and character that is *free from* frustration and disappointment, and *free to do* whatever it wants to do, because it wishes for nothing that falls outside its own power to achieve.

Translating Epictetus

My goal in translating Epictetus has been to minimize the distance between his ancient Greek and contemporary English. Up to a point this is easy because his conversational manner and short sentences suit our modern idiom. He avoids complex sentence structure, as we are taught to do, and it is not difficult to find everyday equivalents to most of his vocabulary. He does use a few technical terms drawn from philosophical jargon, as I explain in the glossary. In rendering these words, for instance *prohairesis* by "will," or *phantasia* by "impression," I explain that other translations of them are possible. What should matter to readers of this or any other version is not word-for-word correspondence but the closest possible representation of the thoughts and intention of the original. While Epictetus follows the convention of his time in using singular masculine pronouns for some of his generalizations, his use of them is not marked or specifically male in reference. Wherever possible I indicate that neutrality by translating the Greek "he" or "him" by "they" or "them."

The difficulties I have encountered in translating Epictetus are not lexical but stylistic and rhetorical. On the surface his Greek is simple and transparent, but these qualities do not emerge in a stream of consciousness, as it were. Antithesis, balance, and rhythm are constant features of the *Encheiridion*, as also are imperatives, numerical grouping of phrases, alliteration, and internal rhyme. It is a challenge to convey all of these qualities in an idiomatic translation. My hope is to capture enough of them to ensure that you are in touch not with my mind but the mind of Epictetus.

I have benefited greatly from consulting all the previous translations that I list under *Further Reading*. Each of them is a conscientious rendering of the original. They differ in style, according to their dates, but hardly or rarely in accuracy. Since novelty for its own sake is not a translator's virtue, the words I choose sometimes coincide with a predecessor's version, and I encourage readers of this book to make comparisons. It is fitting to recall that the first person to make a complete English translation of Epictetus was Elizabeth Carter (1717–1806; see Long 2002, 261). Her work remained standard prior to the Loeb translation by William Oldfather (1925–1928), and it forms the basis of Robin Hard's Everyman version (1995).

ABOUT THE *ENCHEIRIDION*

Arrian (p. xii), to whom we owe the extant works of Epictetus, described the *Encheiridion* as "a selection from Epictetus's speeches containing those that are most timely and most essential to philosophy, and which most stir the soul" (Britain and Brennan 2002, vol. 1, p. 38). This information comes to us from Simplicius, a Platonist philosopher and commentator on Aristotle, who composed a commentary on the text in the sixth century AD, treating it anachronistically as an introduction to Platonism. In the heyday of medieval monasticism, the *Encheiridion* was adapted and paraphrased to suit the needs of Christians (Boter 1999). No fewer than fifty-nine Greek manuscripts attest to the work's early popularity.

ABOUT THE *ENCHEIRIDION*

As a book title, *encheiridion* was not Arrian's invention. The Greek word *cheir* means hand, and an *encheiridion* is literally a little thing for carrying in the hand. The word had been previously used by an Epicurean philosopher to describe a "handy" collection of subject matter. In choosing the word *encheiridion* for his compendium of Epictetus, Arrian's meaning can be largely conveyed by "handbook" or "manual," but I prefer to keep the Greek word. In its earliest usage *encheiridion* refers to a hand-knife or dagger. Arrian may have wished to suggest that connotation of the work's defensive or protective function. It fits his admonition at the beginning and end of the text to keep Epictetus's message "to hand" (*procheiron*). In obvious imitation, Erasmus in 1501 published a work in Latin with the title *Enchiridion militis Christiani* (A Christian Soldier's Manual).

The fifty-three sections of the *Encheiridion* range in length from essays of several hundred words (23, 24, 29) and a long list of do's and dont's (33) to a mere couple of sentences (37, 41, 50). Each section is self-contained, but the collection as a whole has a discernible structure. The first passage, detailing the *things up to us or not up to us*, is clearly introductory and expository. Item 53 with its admonitory quotations rounds off the whole. Near the middle, at section 22, Epictetus shifts his focus from general advice on securing freedom and tranquility to specific counsel for would-be philosophers. He does not call these addressees Stoics, probably because his main concern is not school affiliation but the lifestyle that any philosopher worthy of the name should commit to—a manner of life that is demanding and austere but also modest and unostentatious. However, some of these later sections (e.g.,

36, 42, 45, 49, and 52) allude to specific Stoic doctrines and terminology, as I explain in the glossary.

In the *Discourses,* as will be seen from the excerpts of them in this book, Epictetus often writes in a dialogical style. Section 24 of the *Encheiridion* is written like that, and section 29 repeats *Discourses* 3.15 more or less word for word. In general, however, the *Encheiridion* is more peremptory than the *Discourses* and less discursive ("keep this in mind," "you will have to do that" etc.). Even so, when the sections are read in sequence, a consistent philosophy of life emerges, grounded in the initial postulates concerning the kind of freedom made available by the Stoic view of nature. I recommend readers to spot the implicit arguments that Epictetus constantly employs by his use of conditional clauses: "if you want this, then the consequence will be that," etc.

ABOUT THE *ENCHEIRIDION*

Unlike many ancient Greek books, the transmission of Epictetus's work is free from serious contamination and scribal error for the most part. My translation of the *Encheiridion* largely follows Oldfather's Greek text of the Loeb Classical Library edition (1925–1928), itself based on the edition of Schenkl (1916). Oldfather's text is reprinted here with permission of Harvard University Press. In a few instances, I follow the edition of Boter (1999) in my translation of a word or a phrase, as indicated with the mark +. These changes are indicated in the same way in the Greek text. My excerpts from the *Discourses* reproduce the Loeb Classical Library text without any changes.

In the translation I append the mark * to the first occurrence of words that are explained in the glossary.

HOW TO BE FREE

1. Τῶν ὄντων τὰ μέν ἐστιν ἐφ᾽ ἡμῖν, τὰ δὲ οὐκ ἐφ᾽ ἡμῖν. ἐφ᾽ ἡμῖν μὲν ὑπόληψις, ὁρμή, ὄρεξις, ἔκκλισις καὶ ἑνὶ λόγῳ ὅσα ἡμέτερα ἔργα· οὐκ ἐφ᾽ ἡμῖν δὲ τὸ σῶμα, ἡ κτῆσις, δόξαι, ἀρχαὶ καὶ ἑνὶ λόγῳ ὅσα οὐχ ἡμέτερα ἔργα. καὶ τὰ μὲν ἐφ᾽ ἡμῖν ἐστὶ φύσει ἐλεύθερα, ἀκώλυτα, ἀπαραπόδιστα, τὰ δὲ οὐκ ἐφ᾽ ἡμῖν ἀσθενή, δοῦλα, κωλυτά, ἀλλότρια. μέμνησο οὖν, ὅτι, ἐὰν τὰ φύσει δοῦλα ἐλεύθερα οἰηθῇς καὶ τὰ ἀλλότρια ἴδια, ἐμποδισθήσῃ, πενθήσεις, ταραχθήσῃ, μέμψῃ καὶ θεοὺς καὶ ἀνθρώπους, ἐὰν δὲ τὸ σὸν μόνον οἰηθῇς σὸν εἶναι, τὸ δὲ ἀλλότριον, ὥσπερ ἐστίν, ἀλλότριον, οὐδείς σε ἀναγκάσει οὐδέποτε, οὐδείς σε κωλύσει, οὐ μέμψῃ οὐδένα, οὐκ ἐγκαλέσεις τινί, ἄκων πράξεις οὐδὲ ἕν, + οὐδείς σε βλάψει,+ ἐχθρὸν οὐχ ἕξεις, οὐδὲ γὰρ βλαβερόν τι πείσῃ.

The *Encheiridion*

1. Some things in the world are up to us, while others are not. Up to us are our faculties of judgment, *motivation, *desire, and *aversion—in short, everything that is our own doing. Not up to us are our body and property, our reputations, and our official positions—in short, everything that is not our own doing. Moreover, the things up to us are naturally free, unimpeded, and unconstrained, while the things not up to us are powerless, servile, impeded, and not our own. Keep this in mind then: if you think things naturally servile are free and that things not our own are ours, you will be frustrated, pained, and troubled, and you will find fault with gods and men. But if you think you own only what is yours, and that you do not own what is not yours, as you really don't, no

Τηλικούτων οὖν ἐφιέμενος μέμνησο, ὅτι οὐ δεῖ μετρίως κεκινημένον ἅπτεσθαι αὐτῶν, ἀλλὰ τὰ μὲν ἀφιέναι παντελῶς, τὰ δ' ὑπερτίθεσθαι πρὸς τὸ παρόν. ἐὰν δὲ καὶ ταῦτ' ἐθέλῃς καὶ ἄρχειν καὶ πλουτεῖν, τυχὸν μὲν οὐδ' αὐτῶν τούτων τεύξῃ διὰ τὸ καὶ τῶν προτέρων ἐφίεσθαι, πάντως γε μὴν ἐκείνων ἀποτεύξῃ, δι' ὧν μόνων ἐλευθερία καὶ εὐδαιμονία περιγίνεται.

Εὐθὺς οὖν πάσῃ φαντασίᾳ τραχείᾳ μελέτα ἐπιλέγειν ὅτι " φαντασία εἶ καὶ οὐ πάντως τὸ φαινόμενον." ἔπειτα ἐξέταζε αὐτὴν καὶ δοκίμαζε τοῖς κανόσι τούτοις οἷς ἔχεις, πρώτῳ δὲ τούτῳ καὶ μάλιστα, πότερον περὶ τὰ ἐφ' ἡμῖν ἐστιν ἢ περὶ τὰ οὐκ ἐφ' ἡμῖν· κἂν περί τι τῶν οὐκ ἐφ' ἡμῖν ᾖ, πρόχειρον ἔστω τὸ διότι " οὐδὲν πρὸς ἐμέ."

one will ever put pressure on you, no one will impede you, you will not reproach anyone, you will not blame anyone, you will not do a single thing reluctantly, +no one will harm you, you will have no enemy,+ because nothing harmful will happen to you.

Keep in mind, then, that you have to be highly motivated if you want to achieve such great goals. You will have to forego some things completely, and postpone others for the present. But if you want both at the same time—the things that are really yours plus prominence and wealth in addition—you will probably not get even the latter because of wanting the former as well, and you certainly will not get the former, which are the only way to secure freedom and happiness.

Right now, then, make it your habit to tell every jarring thought or *impression: "You are just an appearance and in no way the real

2. Μέμνησο, ὅτι ὀρέξεως ἐπαγγελία
ἐπιτυχία οὗ ὀρέγῃ, ἐκκλίσεως ἐπαγγελία τὸ μὴ
περιπεσεῖν ἐκείνῳ ὃ ἐκκλίνεται, καὶ ὁ μὲν ἐν
ὀρέξει ἀποτυγχάνων ἀτυχής, ὁ δὲ ἐν ἐκκλίσει
περιπίπτων δυστυχής. ἂν μὲν οὖν μόνα ἐκκλίνῃς
τὰ παρὰ φύσιν τῶν ἐπὶ σοί, οὐδενί, ὧν ἐκκλίνεις,
περιπεσῇ· νόσον δ' ἂν ἐκκλίνῃς ἢ θάνατον ἢ
πενίαν, δυστυχήσεις. ἆρον οὖν τὴν ἔκκλισιν ἀπὸ
πάντων τῶν οὐκ ἐφ' ἡμῖν καὶ μετάθες ἐπὶ τὰ
παρὰ φύσιν τῶν ἐφ' ἡμῖν. τὴν ὄρεξιν δὲ παντελῶς

thing." Next, examine it and test it by these rules that you have. First and foremost: does it involve the things up to us, or the things not up to us? And if it involves one of the things not up to us, have the following response to hand: "Not my business."

2. Keep in mind that desire presumes your getting what you want and that aversion presumes your avoiding what you don't want, and that not getting what we want makes us unfortunate, while encountering what we don't want makes us miserable. So if, among the *things contrary to nature *you restrict aversion to those that are up to you, you will experience none of the things you don't want, but if you are averse to sickness or death or poverty, you will be miserable. So move aversion away from everything that is not up to us and transfer it to the things contrary to nature that are up to

ἐπὶ τοῦ παρόντος ἄνελε· ἄν τε γὰρ ὀρέγῃ τῶν
οὐκ ἐφ' ἡμῖν τινός, ἀτυχεῖν ἀνάγκη, τῶν τε ἐφ'
ἡμῖν, ὅσων ὀρέγεσθαι καλὸν ἄν, οὐδὲν οὐδέπω
σοι πάρεστι. μόνῳ δὲ τῷ ὁρμᾶν καὶ ἀφορμᾶν
χρῶ, κούφως μέντοι καὶ μεθ' ὑπεξαιρέσεως καὶ
ἀνειμένως.

3. Ἐφ' ἑκάστου τῶν ψυχαγωγούντων ἢ χρείαν
παρεχόντων ἢ στεργομένων μέμνησο ἐπιλέγειν,
ὁποῖόν ἐστιν, ἀπὸ τῶν σμικροτάτων ἀρξάμενος.
ἂν χύτραν στέργῃς, ὅτι "ἀχύτραν στέργω "·
κατεαγείσης γὰρ αὐτῆς οὐ ταραχθήσῃ. ἂν παιδίον
σαυτοῦ καταφιλῇς ἢ γυναῖκα, ὅτι ἄνθρωπον
καταφιλεῖς· ἀποθανόντος γὰρ οὐ ταραχθήσῃ.

us. As for desire, give it up completely for the time being. Otherwise, if you desire any of the things that are not up to us, you are bound to be unfortunate, while none of the things up to us, which it would be fine to desire, will be available to you. Confine yourself to motivation and disinclination, and apply these attitudes lightly, with *reservation and without straining.

3. In the case of everything that attracts you or has its uses or that you are fond of, keep in mind to tell yourself what it is like, starting with the most trivial things. If you are fond of a jug, say: "I am fond of a jug." Then, if it is broken, you will not be troubled. When you kiss your little child or your wife, say that you are kissing a human being. Then, if one of them dies, you will not be troubled.

4. Ὅταν ἅπτεσθαί τινος ἔργου μέλλῃς,
ὑπομίμνησκε σεαυτόν, ὁποῖόν ἐστι τὸ ἔργον.
ἐὰν λουσόμενος ἀπίῃς, πρόβαλλε σεαυτῷ τὰ
γινόμενα ἐν βαλανείῳ, τοὺς ἀπορραίνοντας,
τοὺς ἐγκρουομένους, τοὺς λοιδοροῦντας, τοὺς
κλέπτοντας. καὶ οὕτως ἀσφαλέστερον ἅψῃ
τοῦ ἔργου, ἐὰν ἐπιλέγῃς εὐθὺς ὅτι " λούσασθαι
θέλω καὶ τὴν ἐμαυτοῦ προαίρεσιν κατὰ φύσιν
ἔχουσαν τηρῆσαι." καὶ ὡσαύτως ἐφ᾽ ἑκάστου
ἔργου. οὕτω γὰρ ἄν τι πρὸς τὸ λούσασθαι γένηται
ἐμποδών, πρόχειρον ἔσται διότι " ἀλλ᾽ οὐ τοῦτο
ἤθελον μόνον, ἀλλὰ καὶ τὴν ἐμαυτοῦ προαίρεσιν
κατὰ φύσιν ἔχουσαν τηρῆσαι· οὐ τηρήσω δέ, ἐὰν
ἀγανακτῶ πρὸς τὰ γινόμενα."

5. Ταράσσει τοὺς ἀνθρώπους οὐ τὰ πράγματα,
ἀλλὰ τὰ περὶ τῶν πραγμάτων δόγματα· οἷον
ὁ θάνατος οὐδὲν δεινόν, ἐπεὶ καὶ Σωκράτει ἂν

4. Whenever you are about to start on some activity, remind yourself what the activity is like. If you go out to bathe, picture what happens at a bathhouse—the people there who splash you or jostle you or talk rudely or steal your things. In this way you will be more prepared to start on the activity, by telling yourself at the outset: "I want to bathe, and I also want to keep my *will *in harmony with nature." Make this your practice in every activity. Then, if anything happens that gets in the way of your bathing, you will have the following response available: "Well, this was not the only thing I wanted; I also wanted to keep my will in harmony with nature. I shall not do that if I get angry about what is happening."

5. It is not things themselves that trouble people, but their opinions about things. Death, for instance, is nothing terrible (otherwise, it

ἐφαίνετο, ἀλλὰ τὸ δόγμα τὸ περὶ τοῦ θανάτου, διότι δεινόν, ἐκεῖνο τὸ δεινόν ἐστιν. ὅταν οὖν ἐμποδιζώμεθα ἢ ταρασσώμεθα ἢ λυπώμεθα, μηδέποτε ἄλλον αἰτιώμεθα, ἀλλ' ἑαυτούς, τοῦτ' ἔστι τὰ ἑαυτῶν δόγματα. ἀπαιδεύτου ἔργον τὸ ἄλλοις ἐγκαλεῖν, ἐφ' οἷς αὐτὸς πράσσει κακῶς· ἠργμένου παιδεύεσθαι τὸ ἑαυτῷ· πεπαιδευμένου τὸ μήτε ἄλλῳ μήτε ἑαυτῷ.

6. Ἐπὶ μηδενὶ ἐπαρθῇς ἀλλοτρίῳ προτερήματι. εἰ ὁ ἵππος ἐπαιρόμενος ἔλεγεν ὅτι " καλός εἰμι," οἰστὸν ἂν ἦν· σὺ δέ, ὅταν λέγῃς ἐπαιρόμενος ὅτι " ἵππον καλὸν ἔχω," ἴσθι, ὅτι ἐπὶ ἵππου ἀγαθῷ ἐπαίρῃ. τί οὖν ἐστὶ σόν ; χρῆσις φαντασιῶν. ὥσθ', ὅταν ἐν χρήσει φαντασιῶν κατὰ φύσιν σχῇς,

would have appeared that way to *Socrates as well), but the terrible thing is the opinion that death is terrible. So whenever we are frustrated, or troubled, or pained, let us never hold anyone responsible except ourselves, meaning our own opinions. Uneducated people blame others when they are doing badly. Those whose education is underway blame themselves. But a fully educated person blames no one, neither himself nor anyone else.

6. Don't preen yourself on any distinction that is not your own. If the preening horse should say "I am beautiful," it would be acceptable. But when you are preening and say, "I have a beautiful horse," admit that you are preening yourself on a good quality that belongs to the horse. What, then, is your own? The management of *impressions. So whenever you are in harmony with nature

τηνικαῦτα ἐπάρθητι· τότε γὰρ ἐπὶ σῷ τινὶ ἀγαθῷ
ἐπαρθήσῃ.

7. Καθάπερ ἐν πλῷ τοῦ πλοίου καθορμισθέντος
εἰ ἐξέλθοις ὑδρεύσασθαι, ὁδοῦ μὲν πάρεργον
καὶ κοχλίδιον ἀναλέξῃ καὶ βολβάριον, τετάσθαι
δὲ δεῖ τὴν διάνοιαν ἐπὶ τὸ πλοῖον καὶ συνεχῶς
ἐπιστρέφεσθαι, μή ποτε ὁ κυβερνήτης καλέσῃ,
κἂν καλέσῃ, πάντα ἐκεῖνα ἀφιέναι, ἵνα μὴ
δεδεμένος ἐμβληθῇς ὡς τὰ πρόβατα· οὕτω καὶ ἐν
τῷ βίῳ, ἐὰν διδῶται ἀντὶ βολβαρίου καὶ κοχλιδίου
γυναικάριον καὶ παιδίον, οὐδὲν κωλύσει· ἐὰν
δὲ ὁ κυβερνήτης καλέσῃ, τρέχε ἐπὶ τὸ πλοῖον
ἀφεὶς ἐκεῖνα ἅπαντα μηδὲ ἐπιστρεφόμενος. ἐὰν
δὲ γέρων ᾖς, μηδὲ ἀπαλλαγῇς ποτὲ τοῦ πλοίου
μακράν, μή ποτε καλοῦντος ἐλλίπῃς.

in the way you perform this function, that's the time to preen yourself; for then you will have a good thing that is your own to preen yourself on.

7. When you are on a voyage and the boat is at anchor, if you disembark to get water, you may pick up a little shellfish and vegetable on the way, but you need to keep your mind fixed on the boat and keep turning around in case the *captain calls; and if he does call, you must drop all those things, to avoid being tied up and stowed on board like the sheep. That's how it is in life too. If you are given a little wife and child, instead of a little vegetable and shellfish, that will not be a problem. But if the captain calls you, run to the boat and leave all those things without even turning around. And if you are old, never go far from the boat in case you are missing when he calls.

8. Μὴ ζήτει τὰ γινόμενα γίνεσθαι ὡς θέλεις, ἀλλὰ θέλε τὰ γινόμενα ὡς γίνεται καὶ εὐροήσεις.

9. Νόσος σώματός ἐστιν ἐμπόδιον, προαιρέσεως δὲ οὔ, ἐὰν μὴ αὐτὴ θέλῃ. χώλανσις σκέλους ἐστὶν ἐμπόδιον, προαιρέσεως δὲ οὔ. καὶ τοῦτο ἐφ᾽ ἑκάστου τῶν ἐμπιπτόντων ἐπίλεγε· εὑρήσεις γὰρ αὐτὸ ἄλλου τινὸς ἐμπόδιον, σὸν δὲ οὔ.

10. Ἐφ᾽ ἑκάστου τῶν προσπιπτόντων μέμνησο ἐπιστρέφων ἐπὶ σεαυτὸν ζητεῖν, τίνα δύναμιν ἔχεις πρὸς τὴν χρῆσιν αὐτοῦ. ἐὰν καλὸν ἴδῃς ἢ καλήν, εὑρήσεις δύναμιν πρὸς ταῦτα ἐγκράτειαν· ἐὰν πόνος προσφέρηται, εὑρήσεις καρτερίαν· ἂν λοιδορία, εὑρήσεις ἀνεξικακίαν. καὶ οὕτως ἐθιζόμενόν σε οὐ συναρπάσουσιν αἱ φαντασίαι.

8. Don't ask for things to happen as you would like them to, but wish them to happen as they actually do, and you will be all right.

9. Sickness is an impediment to the body, but not to the will unless the will wants to be impeded. Lameness is an impediment to the leg, but not to the will. If you tell yourself this at every occurrence, you will find the impediment is to something else but not to yourself.

10. In all circumstances keep in mind to turn in to yourself and ask what resources you have for dealing with these things. If you see a good-looking man or woman, you will find self-control the appropriate power; if pain afflicts you, you will find endurance; if rudeness, you will find patience. By developing these habits, you will not be carried away by your first impressions.

11. Μηδέποτε ἐπὶ μηδενὸς εἴπῃς ὅτι " ἀπώλεσα αὐτό," ἀλλ᾽ ὅτι " ἀπέδωκα." τὸ παιδίον ἀπέθανεν; ἀπεδόθη. ἡ γυνὴ ἀπέθανεν; ἀπεδόθη. " τὸ χωρίον ἀφῃρέθην." οὐκοῦν καὶ τοῦτο ἀπεδόθη. " ἀλλὰ κακὸς ὁ ἀφελόμενος." τί δὲ σοὶ μέλει, διὰ τίνος σε ὁ δοὺς ἀπήτησε; μέχρι δ᾽ ἂν +διδῶται+, ὡς +ἀλλοτρίων αὐτῶν+ ἐπιμελοῦ, ὡς τοῦ πανδοχείου οἱ παριόντες.

12. Εἰ προκόψαι θέλεις, ἄφες τοὺς τοιούτους ἐπιλογισμούς. " ἐὰν ἀμελήσω τῶν ἐμῶν, οὐχ ἕξω διατροφάς "· " ἐὰν μὴ κολάσω τὸν παῖδα, πονηρὸς ἔσται." κρεῖσσον γὰρ λιμῷ ἀποθανεῖν ἄλυπον καὶ ἄφοβον γενόμενον ἢ ζῆν ἐν ἀφθόνοις ταρασσόμενον. κρεῖττον δὲ +καὶ+ τὸν παῖδα κακὸν εἶναι ἢ σὲ κακοδαίμονα. ἄρξαι τοιγαροῦν ἀπὸ τῶν σμικρῶν. ἐκχεῖται τὸ

11. Never say about anything, "I have lost it"; but say, "I have returned it." Has your little child died? "It has been returned." Has your wife died? "She has been returned." "I have been robbed of my land." No, that has been returned as well. "But it was a bad person who stole it." Why are you bothered about the individual the *donor used to demand its return? As long as these things +are given+ to you, take care of them as +things that are not your own, + just as travelers treat their lodging.

12. If you want to make *progress, dismiss this kind of reasoning: "If I neglect my business, I will have nothing to live on," or "If I don't punish my slave, he will be no good." It is better to starve to death in a calm and confident state of mind than to live anxiously amidst abundance. And it is better +also+ for your slave to be bad than for you to be unhappy. So

ἐλάδιον, κλέπτεται τὸ οἰνάριον· ἐπίλεγε ὅτι
"τοσούτου πωλεῖται ἀπάθεια, τοσούτου
ἀταραξία"· προῖκα δὲ οὐδὲν περιγίνεται. ὅταν
δὲ καλῇς τὸν παῖδα, ἐνθυμοῦ, ὅτι δύναται μὴ
ὑπακοῦσαι ἢ ὑπακούσας μηδὲν ποιῆσαι ὧν
θέλεις· ἀλλ' οὐχ οὕτως ἐστὶν αὐτῷ καλῶς, ἵνα ἐπ'
ἐκείνῳ ᾖ τὸ σὲ μὴ ταραχθῆναι.

13. Εἰ προκόψαι θέλεις, ὑπόμεινον ἕνεκα
τῶν ἐκτὸς ἀνόητος δόξας καὶ ἠλίθιος, μηδὲν
βούλου δοκεῖν ἐπίστασθαι· κἂν δόξῃς τις εἶναί
τισιν, ἀπίστει σεαυτῷ. ἴσθι γὰρ ὅτι οὐ ῥᾴδιον
τὴν προαίρεσιν τὴν σεαυτοῦ κατὰ φύσιν
ἔχουσαν φυλάξαι καὶ τὰ ἐκτός, ἀλλὰ τοῦ ἑτέρου
ἐπιμελούμενον τοῦ ἑτέρου ἀμελῆσαι πᾶσα
ἀνάγκη.

make a start with the little things, like some oil being spilled or some wine being stolen. Then tell yourself: "This is the price one pays for not getting worked up, the price for *tranquility. Nothing comes free of charge." When you summon your slave, reflect that he is quite capable of not responding, or if he does respond that he may do none of the things you want. In any case he is too unimportant for your own tranquility to depend on him.

13. If you want to make progress, don't mind appearing foolish and silly where outward things are concerned, and don't wish to appear an expert. Even if some people think you are somebody, distrust yourself. It is not easy, you can be sure, to keep your own will in harmony with nature and simultaneously secure outward things. If you care about the one, you are completely bound to neglect the other.

14. Ἐὰν θέλῃς τὰ τέκνα σου καὶ τὴν γυναῖκα καὶ τοὺς φίλους σου +πάντως+ ζῆν, ἠλίθιος εἶ· τὰ γὰρ μὴ ἐπὶ σοὶ θέλεις ἐπὶ σοὶ εἶναι καὶ τὰ ἀλλότρια σὰ εἶναι· οὕτω κἂν τὸν παῖδα θέλῃς μὴ ἁμαρτάνειν, μωρὸς εἶ· θέλεις γὰρ τὴν κακίαν μὴ εἶναι κακίαν, ἀλλ' ἄλλο τι. ἐὰν δὲ θέλῃς ὀρεγόμενος μὴ ἀποτυγχάνειν, τοῦτο δύνασαι. τοῦτο οὖν ἄσκει, ὃ δύνασαι. κύριος ἑκάστου ἐστὶν ὁ τῶν ὑπ' ἐκείνου θελομένων ἢ μὴ θελομένων ἔχων τὴν ἐξουσίαν εἰς τὸ περιποιῆσαι ἢ ἀφελέσθαι. ὅστις οὖν ἐλεύθερος εἶναι βούλεται, μήτε θελέτω τι μήτε φευγέτω τι τῶν ἐπ' ἄλλοις· εἰ δὲ μή, δουλεύειν ἀνάγκη.

15. Μέμνησο, ὅτι ὡς ἐν συμποσίῳ σε δεῖ ἀναστρέφεσθαι. περιφερόμενον γέγονέ τι κατὰ σέ· ἐκτείνας τὴν χεῖρα κοσμίως μετάλαβε.

14. If you want your children and your wife and friends to survive +no matter what, + you are silly; for you are wanting things to be up to you that are not up to you, and things to be your own that are not your own. You are just as foolish if you want your slave to make no mistakes; for you are wanting inferiority not to be a flaw but something else. But if your wish is not to be frustrated in your desires, this is in your power. Train yourself, then, in this power that you do have. Our master is anyone who has the power to implement or prevent the things that we want or don't want. Whoever wants to be free, therefore, should wish for nothing or avoid nothing that is up to other people. Failing that, one is bound to be a slave.

15. Keep in mind that you should always behave as you would do at a banquet. Something comes around to you; stretch out your hand

παρέρχεται· μὴ κάτεχε. οὔπω ἥκει· μὴ ἐπίβαλλε
πόρρω τὴν ὄρεξιν, ἀλλὰ περίμενε, μέχρις ἂν
γένηται κατὰ σέ. οὕτω πρὸς τέκνα, οὕτω πρὸς
γυναῖκα, οὕτω πρὸς ἀρχάς, οὕτω πρὸς πλοῦτον·
καὶ ἔσῃ ποτὲ ἄξιος τῶν θεῶν συμπότης. ἂν δὲ
καὶ παρατεθέντων σοι μὴ λάβῃς, ἀλλ᾽ ὑπερίδῃς,
τότε οὐ μόνον συμπότης τῶν θεῶν ἔσῃ, ἀλλὰ
καὶ συνάρχων. οὕτω γὰρ ποιῶν Διογένης καὶ
Ἡράκλειτος καὶ οἱ ὅμοιοι ἀξίως θεῖοί τε ἦσαν καὶ
ἐλέγοντο.

16. Ὅταν κλαίοντα ἴδῃς τινὰ ἐν πένθει ἢ
ἀποδημοῦντος τέκνου ἢ ἀπολωλεκότα τὰ
ἑαυτοῦ, πρόσεχε μή σε ἡ φαντασία συναρπάσῃ
ὡς ἐν κακοῖς ὄντος αὐτοῦ τοῖς ἐκτός, ἀλλ᾽
εὐθὺς ἔστω πρόχειρον ὅτι " τοῦτον θλίβει οὐ
τὸ συμβεβηκός (ἄλλον γὰρ οὐ θλίβει), ἀλλὰ τὸ
δόγμα τὸ περὶ τούτου." μέχρι μέντοι λόγου μὴ

and politely take a portion. It passes on; don't try to stop it. It has not come yet; don't let your appetite run ahead, but wait till the portion reaches you. If you act like this toward your children, your wife, your public positions, and your wealth, you will be worthy one day to dine with the *gods. And if you don't even take things, when they are put before you, but pass them by, you will not only dine with the gods but also share their rule. It was by acting like that that *Diogenes and *Heracles and others like them were deservedly divine and called so.

16. Whenever you see someone grieving at the departure of their child or the loss of their property, take care not to be carried away by the impression that they are in dire external straits, but at once have the following thought available: "What is crushing these people is not the event (since there are other people it does

ὄκνει συμπεριφέρεσθαι αὐτῷ, κἂν οὕτω τύχῃ, καὶ
συνεπιστενάξαι· πρόσεχε μέντοι μὴ καὶ ἔσωθεν
στενάξῃς.

17. Μέμνησο, ὅτι ὑποκριτὴς εἶ δράματος,
οἵου ἂν θέλῃ ὁ διδάσκαλος· ἂν βραχύ, βραχέος·
ἂν μακρόν, μακροῦ· ἂν πτωχὸν ὑποκρίνασθαί
σε θέλῃ, ἵνα καὶ τοῦτον εὐφυῶς ὑποκρίνῃ· ἂν
χωλόν, ἂν ἄρχοντα, ἂν ἰδιώτην. σὸν γὰρ τοῦτ᾽
ἔστι, τὸ δοθὲν ὑποκρίνασθαι πρόσωπον καλῶς·
ἐκλέξασθαι δ᾽ αὐτὸ ἄλλου.

18. Κόραξ ὅταν μὴ αἴσιον κεκράγῃ, μὴ
συναρπαζέτω σε ἡ φαντασία· ἀλλ᾽ εὐθὺς διαίρει
παρὰ σεαυτῷ καὶ λέγε ὅτι " τούτων ἐμοὶ οὐδὲν
ἐπισημαίνεται, ἀλλ᾽ ἢ τῷ σωματίῳ μου ἢ τῷ
κτησειδίῳ μου ἢ τῷ δοξαρίῳ μου ἢ τοῖς τέκνοις ἢ

not crush) but their opinion about it." Don't hesitate, however, to sympathize with them in words and even maybe share their groans, but take care not to groan inwardly as well.

17. Keep in mind that you are an actor in a play that is just the way the *producer wants it to be. It is short, if that is his wish, or long, if he wants it long. If he wants you to act the part of a beggar, see that you play it skillfully; and similarly if the part is to be a cripple, or an official, or a private person. Your job is to put on a splendid performance of the role you have been given, but selecting the role is the job of someone else.

18. Whenever a raven croaks ominously, don't let the impression carry you away, but straightaway discriminate within yourself, and say: "None of this is a warning to me; it only concerns my feeble body or my tiny estate or

τῇ γυναικί. ἐμοὶ δὲ πάντα αἴσια σημαίνεται, ἐὰν ἐγὼ θέλω· ὅ τι γὰρ ἂν τούτων ἀποβαίνῃ, ἐπ' ἐμοί ἐστιν ὠφεληθῆναι ἀπ' αὐτοῦ."

19. Ἀνίκητος εἶναι δύνασαι, ἐὰν εἰς μηδένα ἀγῶνα καταβαίνῃς, ὃν οὐκ ἔστιν ἐπὶ σοὶ νικῆσαι. 2 ὅρα μήποτε ἰδών τινα προτιμώμενον ἢ μέγα δυνάμενον ἢ ἄλλως εὐδοκιμοῦντα μακαρίσῃς, ὑπὸ τῆς φαντασίας συναρπασθείς. ἐὰν γὰρ ἐν τοῖς ἐφ' ἡμῖν ἡ οὐσία τοῦ ἀγαθοῦ ᾖ, οὔτε φθόνος οὔτε ζηλοτυπία χώραν ἔχει· σύ τε αὐτὸς οὐ στρατηγός, οὐ πρύτανις ἢ ὕπατος εἶναι θελήσεις, ἀλλ' ἐλεύθερος. μία δὲ ὁδὸς πρὸς τοῦτο, καταφρόνησις τῶν οὐκ ἐφ' ἡμῖν.

20. Μέμνησο, ὅτι οὐχ ὁ λοιδορῶν ἢ ὁ τύπτων ὑβρίζει, ἀλλὰ τὸ δόγμα τὸ περὶ τούτων ὡς

my paltry reputation or my children or my wife. But to myself all predictions are favorable if I wish them to be, since it is up to me to benefit from the outcome, whatever it may be."

19. You can always win if you only enter competitions where winning is up to you. When you see someone honored ahead of you or holding great power or being highly esteemed in another way, be careful never to be carried away by the impression and judge the person to be happy. For if the essence of goodness consists in things that are up to us, there is room for neither envy nor jealousy, and you yourself will not want to be a *praetor or a senator or a consul, but to be free. The only way to achieve this is by despising the things that are not up to us.

20. Keep in mind that what injures you is not people who are rude or aggressive but your

ὑβριζόντων. ὅταν οὖν ἐρεθίσῃ σέ τις, ἴσθι, ὅτι ἡ
σή σε ὑπόληψις ἠρέθικε. τοιγαροῦν ἐν πρώτοις
πειρῶ ὑπὸ τῆς φαντασίας μὴ συναρπασθῆναι·
ἂν γὰρ ἅπαξ χρόνου καὶ διατριβῆς τύχῃς, ῥᾷον
κρατήσεις σεαυτοῦ.

21. Θάνατος καὶ φυγὴ καὶ πάντα τὰ +ἄλλα τὰ+
δεινὰ φαινόμενα πρὸ ὀφθαλμῶν ἔστω σοι καθ᾽
ἡμέραν, μάλιστα δὲ πάντων ὁ θάνατος· καὶ οὐδὲν
οὐδέποτε οὔτε ταπεινὸν ἐνθυμηθήσῃ οὔτε ἄγαν
ἐπιθυμήσεις τινός.

22. Εἰ φιλοσοφίας ἐπιθυμεῖς, παρασκευάζου
αὐτόθεν ὡς καταγελασθησόμενος, ὡς
καταμωκησομένων σου πολλῶν, ὡς ἐρούντων
ὅτι " ἄφνω φιλόσοφος ἡμῖν ἐπανελήλυθε" καὶ
"πόθεν ἡμῖν αὕτη ἡ ὀφρύς ; " σὺ δὲ ὀφρὺν μὲν μὴ
σχῇς· τῶν δὲ βελτίστων σοι φαινομένων οὕτως
ἔχου, ὡς ὑπὸ τοῦ θεοῦ τεταγμένος εἰς ταύτην τὴν

opinion that they are injuring you. So whenever someone provokes you, be aware that the provocation really comes from your own judgment. Start, then, by trying not to get carried away by the impression. Once you pause and give yourself time, you will more easily control yourself.

21. Set before your eyes every day death and exile and everything +else+ that looks terrible, especially death. Then you will never have any mean thought or be too keen on anything.

22. If you are keen on philosophy, be ready at the outset to be laughed at and mocked by many people with words like "What do you know, he's come back to us as a philosopher!" and "Where did he get that superior look from?" Don't look that way, then, but stick to your views of what is best, as one who has been

χώραν· μέμνησό τε διότι, ἐὰν μὲν ἐμμείνῃς τοῖς
αὐτοῖς, οἱ καταγελῶντές σου τὸ πρότερον οὗτοί
σε ὕστερον θαυμάσονται, ἐὰν δὲ ἡττηθῇς αὐτῶν,
διπλοῦν προσλήψῃ καταγέλωτα.

23. Ἐάν ποτέ σοι γένηται ἔξω στραφῆναι πρὸς
τὸ βούλεσθαι ἀρέσαι τινί, ἴσθι ὅτι ἀπώλεσας τὴν
ἔνστασιν. ἀρκοῦ οὖν ἐν παντὶ τῷ εἶναι φιλόσοφος,
εἰ δὲ καὶ δοκεῖν βούλει, σαυτῷ φαίνου καὶ
+ἱκανὸν ἐστι.+

24. Οὗτοί σε οἱ διαλογισμοὶ μὴ θλιβέτωσαν·
"ἄτιμος ἐγὼ βιώσομαι καὶ οὐδεὶς οὐδαμοῦ." εἰ
γὰρ ἡ ἀτιμία ἐστὶ κακόν +(ὥσπερ ἐστίν)+, οὐ
δύνασαι ἐν κακῷ εἶναι δι' ἄλλον, οὐ μᾶλλον ἢ
ἐν αἰσχρῷ· μή τι οὖν σόν ἐστιν ἔργον τὸ ἀρχῆς

appointed to this place by God. And keep in mind that if you stick to those same views, the people who used to laugh at you will admire you later, but if you lapse from them, you will be a laughingstock for a second time.

23. If you ever find yourself looking for outside approval in order to curry favor, you can be sure that you have lost your way. Be satisfied, then, simply to *be* a philosopher, and if you want people to think of you that way as well, appear so to yourself, and that will be +sufficient.+

24. Don't let yourself be worried by thinking, "My life is going to be without honor, and I will be a nobody everywhere." If lack of honor is something bad +(as it is),+ no one but yourself could be responsible, any more than others could put you in a shameful position. You don't really think it's your job to secure

τυχεῖν ἢ παραληφθῆναι ἐφ' ἑστίασιν ; οὐδαμῶς.
πῶς οὖν ἔτι τοῦτ' ἔστιν ἀτιμία ; πῶς δὲ οὐδεὶς
οὐδαμοῦ ἔσῃ, ὃν ἐν μόνοις εἶναί τινα δεῖ τοῖς
ἐπὶ σοί, ἐν οἷς ἔξεστί σοι εἶναι πλείστου ἀξίῳ ;
ἀλλά σοι οἱ φίλοι ἀβοήθητοι ἔσονται ; τί λέγεις
τὸ ἀβοήθητοι; οὐχ ἕξουσι παρὰ σοῦ κερμάτιον·
οὐδὲ πολίτας Ῥωμαίων αὐτοὺς ποιήσεις. τίς οὖν
σοι εἶπεν, ὅτι ταῦτα τῶν ἐφ' ἡμῖν ἐστίν, οὐχὶ δὲ
ἀλλότρια ἔργα; τίς δὲ δοῦναι δύναται ἑτέρῳ, ἃ μὴ
ἔχει αὐτός ; "κτῆσαι οὖν," φησίν, " ἵνα +καὶ+ ἡμεῖς
ἔχωμεν." εἰ δύναμαι κτήσασθαι τηρῶν ἐμαυτὸν
αἰδήμονα καὶ πιστὸν καὶ μεγαλόφρονα, δείκνυε
τὴν ὁδὸν καὶ κτήσομαι. εἰ δ' ἐμὲ ἀξιοῦτε τὰ ἀγαθὰ
τὰ ἐμαυτοῦ ἀπολέσαι, ἵνα ὑμεῖς τὰ μὴ ἀγαθὰ
περιποιήσησθε, ὁρᾶτε ὑμεῖς, πῶς ἄνισοί ἐστε καὶ

a public office, do you, or be invited to a banquet? "Of course not." How, then, is this still a lack of honor? And how will you be a nobody everywhere, since you need to be somebody only in the things that are up to you, and in them you can be a top person?

"But your friends will lack support?" What do you mean by "lack support"? They won't get a cash handout from you, and you won't make them Roman citizens. But who told you that these things are up to us and not the business of other people? Who can give to another what he doesn't have himself?

"Get money, then," someone says, "so we can have it too." If I can get it and preserve my honor and integrity and moral principles, show me the way, and I will get it. But if you are asking me to lose the *good things that are mine just for you to acquire things that are not good, you can see how unfair you are and how

ἀγνώμονες. τί δὲ καὶ βούλεσθε μᾶλλον ; ἀργύριον
ἢ φίλον πιστὸν καὶ αἰδήμονα ; εἰς τοῦτο οὖν μοι
μᾶλλον συλλαμβάνετε καὶ μή, δι' ὧν ἀποβαλῶ
αὐτὰ ταῦτα, ἐκεῖνά με πράσσειν ἀξιοῦτε.

"Ἀλλ' ἡ πατρίς, ὅσον ἐπ' ἐμοί," φησίν,
"ἀβοήθητος ἔσται." πάλιν, ποίαν καὶ ταύτην
βοήθειαν ; στοὰς οὐχ ἕξει διὰ σὲ οὔτε βαλανεῖα.
καὶ τί τοῦτο ; οὐδὲ γὰρ ὑποδήματα ἔχει διὰ τὸν
χαλκέα οὐδ' ὅπλα διὰ τὸν σκυτέα· ἱκανὸν δέ,
ἐὰν ἕκαστος ἐκπληρώσῃ τὸ ἑαυτοῦ ἔργον. εἰ δὲ
ἄλλον τινὰ αὐτῇ κατεσκεύαζες πολίτην πιστὸν
καὶ αἰδήμονα, οὐδὲν ἂν αὐτὴν ὠφέλεις ; " ναί."
οὐκοῦν οὐδὲ σὺ αὐτὸς ἀνωφελὴς ἂν εἴης αὐτῇ. "
τίνα οὖν ἕξω," φησί, " χώραν ἐν τῇ πόλει ; " ἣν ἂν
δύνῃ φυλάττων ἅμα τὸν πιστὸν καὶ αἰδήμονα. εἰ
δὲ ἐκείνην ὠφελεῖν βουλόμενος ἀποβαλεῖς ταῦτα,
τί ὄφελος ἂν αὐτῇ γένοιο ἀναιδὴς καὶ ἄπιστος
ἀποτελεσθείς ;

ungenerous. What would you rather have—money or a trustworthy and honorable friend? Help me, rather, to maintain this character and do not ask me to do the very things that will make me lose it.

"But my country," someone says, "will lack such support as I could have given." I repeat the question of what support you have in mind. Your country will not have colonnades or public baths because of you. But what does that mean? Your country does not have shoes because of the blacksmith or weapons because of the cobbler? It is enough if each person performs his own job. And if you were to supply your country with another trustworthy and honorable citizen, would you not be doing it a benefit? "Yes, I would." So you yourself would not be of no benefit to your community.

"What position, then, will I hold in it?" Whichever one you *can* have and still preserve

25. +Εἰ+ προετιμήθη σού τις ἐν ἑστιάσει ἢ ἐν προσαγορεύσει ἢ ἐν τῷ παραληφθῆναι εἰς συμβουλίαν ; εἰ μὲν ἀγαθὰ ταῦτά ἐστι, χαίρειν σε δεῖ, ὅτι ἔτυχεν αὐτῶν ἐκεῖνος· εἰ δὲ κακά, μὴ ἄχθου, ὅτι σὺ αὐτῶν οὐκ ἔτυχες· μέμνησο δέ, ὅτι οὐ δύνασαι μὴ ταὐτὰ ποιῶν πρὸς τὸ τυγχάνειν τῶν οὐκ ἐφ᾽ ἡμῖν τῶν ἴσων ἀξιοῦσθαι. πῶς γὰρ ἴσον ἔχειν δύναται ὁ μὴ φοιτῶν ἐπὶ θύρας τινὸς τῷ φοιτῶντι ; ὁ μὴ παραπέμπων τῷ παραπέμποντι ; ὁ μὴ ἐπαινῶν τῷ ἐπαινοῦντι ; ἄδικος οὖν ἔσῃ καὶ ἄπληστος, εἰ μὴ προϊέμενος ταῦτα, ἀνθ᾽ ὧν ἐκεῖνα πιπράσκεται, προῖκα αὐτὰ βουλήσῃ λαμβάνειν.

Ἀλλὰ πόσου πιπράσκονται θρίδακες ; ὀβολοῦ, ἂν οὕτω τύχῃ. ἂν οὖν τις προέμενος τὸν ὀβολὸν λάβῃ θρίδακας, σὺ δὲ μὴ προέμενος μὴ λάβῃς,

your trustworthy and honorable character. But if you lose this character in wanting to benefit your country, and you end up dishonorable and untrustworthy, what benefit would you be?

25. +If+ someone has been placed ahead of you at a banquet or in a reception line or in being called on as a consultant, you should be pleased that he has got these things, if they are good. But if they are bad, don't be upset because you didn't get them. Keep in mind that you cannot expect to get an equal share of the things that are not up to us without doing the same things others have done. If you don't hang out at someone's door or go around with him or flatter him, how can you have the same share of his regard as the person who does these things? If you don't pay the price these things are sold at, and want to get them for free, you would be unfair and greedy.

μὴ οἴου ἔλαττον ἔχειν τοῦ λαβόντος. ὡς γὰρ
ἐκεῖνος ἔχει θρίδακας, οὕτω σὺ τὸν ὀβολόν, ὃν
οὐκ ἔδωκας. τὸν αὐτὸν δὴ τρόπον καὶ ἐνταῦθα. οὐ
παρεκλήθης ἐφ᾽ ἑστίασίν τινος ; οὐ γὰρ ἔδωκας τῷ
καλοῦντι, ὅσου πωλεῖ τὸ δεῖπνον. ἐπαίνου δ᾽ αὐτὸ
πωλεῖ, θεραπείας πωλεῖ. δὸς οὖν τὸ διάφορον, εἴ
σοι λυσιτελεῖ, ὅσου πωλεῖται. εἰ δὲ κἀκεῖνα θέλεις
μὴ προΐεσθαι καὶ ταῦτα λαμβάνειν, ἄπληστος εἶ
καὶ ἀβέλτερος. οὐδὲν οὖν ἔχεις ἀντὶ τοῦ δείπνου;
ἔχεις μὲν οὖν τὸ μὴ ἐπαινέσαι τοῦτον, ὃν οὐκ
ἤθελες, τὸ μὴ ἀνασχέσθαι αὐτοῦ τῶν ἐπὶ τῆς
εἰσόδου.

26. Τὸ βούλημα τῆς φύσεως καταμαθεῖν ἔστιν
ἐξ ὧν οὐ διαφερόμεθα πρὸς ἀλλήλους. οἷον, ὅταν
ἄλλου παιδάριον κατεάξῃ τὸ ποτήριον, πρόχειρον
εὐθὺς λέγειν ὅτι " τῶν γινομένων ἐστίν." ἴσθι

What's the cost of lettuces? An *obol maybe. If someone pays an obol and gets the lettuces, don't think you have less than he has. While he has the lettuces, you have the unspent obol. It's just the same in the cases we are considering. You were not invited to someone's dinner party. That's because you didn't pay the host the price of the dinner. He sells it for flattery, for getting attention. Pay the price it's sold for, then, if you think it's worth it. But if you want to get it without paying up, you are being greedy and stupid. Do you have nothing instead of the dinner? Of course you do. You don't have to flatter the man you didn't want to flatter or to deal with the crowd around his door.

26. *Nature's purpose can be learned from situations that we all agree about. When, for instance, someone else's slave breaks his master's drinking cup, one is instantly ready to say,

οὖν, ὅτι, ὅταν καὶ τὸ σὸν κατεαγῇ, τοιοῦτον εἶναί σε δεῖ, ὁποῖον ὅτε καὶ τὸ τοῦ ἄλλου κατεάγη. οὕτω μετατίθει καὶ ἐπὶ τὰ μείζονα. τέκνον ἄλλου τέθνηκεν ἢ γυνή· οὐδείς ἐστιν ὃς οὐκ ἂν εἴποι ὅτι " ἀνθρώπινον." ἀλλ' ὅταν τὸ αὐτοῦ τινος ἀποθάνῃ, εὐθὺς " οἴμοι, τάλας ἐγώ." ἐχρῆν δὲ μεμνῆσθαι, τί πάσχομεν περὶ ἄλλων αὐτὸ ἀκούσαντες.

27. Ὥσπερ σκοπὸς πρὸς τὸ ἀποτυχεῖν οὐ τίθεται, οὕτως οὐδὲ κακοῦ φύσις ἐν κόσμῳ γίνεται.

28. Εἰ μὲν τὸ σῶμά σού τις ἐπέτρεπε τῷ ἀπαντήσαντι, ἠγανάκτεις ἄν· ὅτι δὲ σὺ τὴν γνώμην τὴν σεαυτοῦ ἐπιτρέπεις τῷ τυχόντι, ἵνα, ἐὰν λοιδορήσηταί σοι, ταραχθῇ ἐκείνη καὶ συγχυθῇ, οὐκ αἰσχύνῃ τούτου ἕνεκα ;

"It's just an accident." So when your own cup gets broken, acknowledge that you should be just the way you were when that happened to the other person's cup. Now apply this rule to more serious things. When someone's child or wife dies, it's normal to say "That's just life." Yet whenever it's one's own family member who dies, the immediate response is "Alas" and "Poor me!" We should remember how we feel when we hear of this happening to other people.

27. No target is set up simply to be missed, and in the same way nothing that occurs in the world is *bad in its own nature as such.

28. If someone in the street were entrusted with your body, you would be furious. Yet you entrust your mind to anyone around who happens to insult you, and allow it to be troubled and confused. Aren't you ashamed of that?

29. Ἑκάστου ἔργου σκόπει τὰ καθηγούμενα καὶ τὰ ἀκόλουθα αὐτοῦ καὶ οὕτως ἔρχου ἐπ' αὐτό. εἰ δὲ μή, τὴν μὲν πρώτην προθύμως ἤξεις ἅτε μηδὲν τῶν ἑξῆς ἐντεθυμημένος, ὕστερον δὲ ἀναφανέντων δυσχερῶν τινῶν αἰσχρῶς ἀποστήσῃ. θέλεις Ὀλύμπια νικῆσαι ; κἀγώ, νὴ τοὺς θεούς· κομψὸν γάρ ἐστιν. ἀλλὰ σκόπει τὰ καθηγούμενα καὶ τὰ ἀκόλουθα καὶ οὕτως ἅπτου τοῦ ἔργου. δεῖ σ' εὐτακτεῖν, ἀναγκοτροφεῖν, ἀπέχεσθαι πεμμάτων, γυμνάζεσθαι πρὸς ἀνάγκην, ἐν ὥρᾳ τεταγμένῃ, ἐν καύματι, ἐν ψύχει, μὴ ψυχρὸν πίνειν, μὴ οἶνον, ὡς ἔτυχεν, ἁπλῶς ὡς ἰατρῷ παραδεδωκέναι σεαυτὸν τῷ ἐπιστάτῃ, εἶτα ἐν τῷ ἀγῶνι παρορύσσεσθαι, ἔστι δὲ ὅτε χεῖρα ἐκβαλεῖν, σφυρὸν στρέψαι, πολλὴν ἁφὴν καταπιεῖν, ἔσθ' ὅτε μαστιγωθῆναι, καὶ μετὰ τούτων πάντων νικηθῆναι.

Ταῦτα ἐπισκεψάμενος, ἂν ἔτι θέλῃς, ἔρχου ἐπὶ τὸ ἀθλεῖν. εἰ δὲ μή, ὡς τὰ παιδία ἀναστραφήσῃ, ἃ νῦν μὲν παλαιστὰς παίζει, νῦν δὲ μονομάχους,

29. In every undertaking, examine its *antecedents and their consequences, and only then proceed to the act itself. If you don't do that, you will start enthusiastically, because you have not thought about any of the next stages; then, when difficulties appear, you will give up and be put to shame. Do you want to win at the Olympics? I do too, of course, because it's a splendid thing. But examine the project from start to finish, and only go in for it after that. You must train, keep a strict diet, stay off pastries, submit to a regular exercise regime each day, summer or winter, drink no cold water and no wine except at appropriate times; in other words, you have to surrender yourself to the trainer just as you would to your doctor. Then in the actual contest you have to *dig in alongside the other contestants, and perhaps dislocate your hand or twist your ankle, swallow a lot of sand, get flogged, and with all of this lose the fight.

νῦν δὲ σαλπίζει, εἶτα τραγῳδεῖ· οὕτω καὶ σὺ νῦν
μὲν ἀθλητής, νῦν δὲ μονομάχος, εἶτα ῥήτωρ,
εἶτα φιλόσοφος, ὅλῃ δὲ τῇ ψυχῇ οὐδέν· ἀλλ' ὡς
πίθηκος πᾶσαν θέαν, ἣν ἂν ἴδῃς, μιμῇ καὶ ἄλλο ἐξ
ἄλλου σοι ἀρέσκει. οὐ γὰρ μετὰ σκέψεως ἦλθες
ἐπί τι οὐδὲ περιοδεύσας, ἀλλ' εἰκῇ καὶ κατὰ
ψυχρὰν ἐπιθυμίαν.

Οὕτω θεασάμενοί τινες φιλόσοφον καὶ
ἀκούσαντες οὕτω τινὸς λέγοντος, ὡς Εὐφράτης
λέγει (καίτοι τίς οὕτω δύναται εἰπεῖν, ὡς
ἐκεῖνος;), θέλουσι καὶ αὐτοὶ φιλοσοφεῖν. ἄνθρωπε,
πρῶτον ἐπίσκεψαι, ὁποῖόν ἐστι τὸ πρᾶγμα· εἶτα

When you have thought about this, go and compete if you still want to. But if you don't think first, you will be acting like children who play at wrestling for a while, then at being gladiators, then trumpeters, and then stage performers. That's what you are like too, now an athlete, next a gladiator, then an orator, now a philosopher but nothing in your self as a whole. You are like a monkey mimicking whatever you see, as one thing after another takes your fancy. You haven't pursued anything with due consideration or after thorough review; you mess about and don't put your heart into things.

It's the way some people who have seen a philosopher and heard one speak like *Euphrates (though no one can really speak like him) want to go in for philosophy themselves. Dear man, think first about what the thing is like, and then study your own nature to see whether

καὶ τὴν σεαυτοῦ φύσιν κατάμαθε, εἰ δύνασαι
βαστάσαι. πένταθλος εἶναι βούλει ἢ παλαιστής ;
ἴδε σεαυτοῦ τοὺς βραχίονας, τοὺς μηρούς, τὴν
ὀσφὺν κατάμαθε. ἄλλος γὰρ πρὸς ἄλλο πέφυκε.
δοκεῖς, ὅτι ταῦτα ποιῶν ὡσαύτως δύνασαι ἐσθίειν,
ὡσαύτως πίνειν, ὁμοίως +ὀργίζεσθαι+, ὁμοίως
δυσαρεστεῖν ; ἀγρυπνῆσαι δεῖ, πονῆσαι, ἀπὸ τῶν
οἰκείων ἀπελθεῖν, ὑπὸ παιδαρίου καταφρονηθῆναι,
ὑπὸ τῶν ἀπαντώντων καταγελασθῆναι, ἐν
παντὶ ἧττον ἔχειν, ἐν τιμῇ, ἐν ἀρχῇ, ἐν δίκῃ, ἐν
πραγματίῳ παντι. ταῦτα ἐπίσκεψαι, εἰ θέλεις
ἀντικαταλλάξασθαι τούτων ἀπάθειαν, ἐλευθερίαν,
ἀταραξίαν· εἰ δὲ μή, μὴ προσάγαγε, μὴ ὡς τὰ
παιδία νῦν φιλόσοφος, ὕστερον δὲ τελώνης,
εἶτα ῥήτωρ, εἶτα ἐπίτροπος Καίσαρος. ταῦτα οὐ
συμφωνεῖ. ἕνα σε δεῖ ἄνθρωπον ἢ ἀγαθὸν ἢ κακὸν
εἶναι· ἢ τὸ ἡγεμονικόν σε δεῖ ἐξεργάζεσθαι τὸ

you are up to it. Do you really want to compete in the pentathlon or the wrestling? If so, you had better study your arms and your thighs and your hips. People differ in what they are naturally suited to. Do you suppose you can go in for philosophy and eat and drink just as you do now or get angry and +irritated+ in the same way? You are going to have to go without sleep, work really hard, stay away from friends and family, be disrespected by a young slave, get mocked by people in the street, and come off worse in rank, office, or courtroom, everywhere in fact. Think about all this and then see whether you want to exchange it for calm, freedom, and tranquility. If not, don't go near philosophy; don't be like children playing first a philosopher, and after that a tax collector, then an orator, and then an imperial official. These professions don't match. You have to be one person, either good or bad. You have

σαυτοῦ ἢ τὰ ἐκτός· ἢ περὶ τὰ ἔσω φιλοτεχνεῖν
ἢ περὶ τὰ ἔξω· τοῦτ᾽ ἔστιν ἢ φιλοσόφου τάξιν
ἐπέχειν ἢ ἰδιώτου.

30. Τὰ καθήκοντα ὡς ἐπίπαν ταῖς σχέσεσι
παραμετρεῖται. πατήρ ἐστιν· ὑπαγορεύεται
ἐπιμελεῖσθαι, παραχωρεῖν ἁπάντων, ἀνέχεσθαι
λοιδοροῦντος, παίοντος. " ἀλλὰ πατὴρ κακός
ἐστι." μή τι οὖν πρὸς ἀγαθὸν πατέρα φύσει
ᾠκειώθης ; ἀλλὰ πρὸς πατέρα. " ὁ ἀδελφὸς
ἀδικεῖ." τήρει τοιγαροῦν τὴν τάξιν τὴν σεαυτοῦ
πρὸς αὐτόν· μηδὲ σκόπει, τί ἐκεῖνος ποιεῖ, ἀλλὰ τί
σοὶ ποιήσαντι κατὰ φύσιν ἕξει ἡ σὴ προαίρεσις.
σὲ γὰρ ἄλλος οὐ βλάψει, ἂν μὴ σὺ θέλῃς· τότε δὲ
ἔσῃ βεβλαμμένος, ὅταν ὑπολάβῃς βλάπτεσθαι.

to work either on your *commanding-faculty or on external things. Either the inner or the outer should be the focus of your efforts, which means adopting the role either of a philosopher or of an ordinary person.

30. *Appropriate actions are largely set by our social relationships. In the case of one's father, this involves looking after him, letting him have his way in everything, and not making a fuss if he is abusive or violent. "But what if he's a bad father? " Do you think you have a *natural affinity only to a good father? "No, just to a father." Suppose your brother treats you badly. In that case, maintain your fraternal relationship to him. Don't think about why he behaves that way but about what you need to do to keep your will in harmony with nature. No one else, in fact, will harm you without your consent; you will be harmed only when you think you

οὕτως οὖν ἀπὸ τοῦ γείτονος, ἀπὸ τοῦ πολίτου,
ἀπὸ τοῦ στρατηγοῦ τὸ καθῆκον εὑρήσεις, ἐὰν τὰς
σχέσεις ἐθίζῃ θεωρεῖν.

31. Τῆς περὶ τοὺς θεοὺς εὐσεβείας ἴσθι ὅτι
τὸ κυριώτατον ἐκεῖνό ἐστιν, ὀρθὰς ὑπολήψεις
περὶ αὐτῶν ἔχειν ὡς ὄντων καὶ διοικούντων τὰ
ὅλα καλῶς καὶ δικαίως, καὶ σαυτὸν εἰς τοῦτο
κατατεταχέναι, τὸ πείθεσθαι αὐτοῖς καὶ εἴκειν
πᾶσι τοῖς γινομένοις καὶ ἀκολουθεῖν ἑκόντα ὡς
ὑπὸ τῆς ἀρίστης γνώμης ἐπιτελουμένοις.
οὕτω γὰρ οὐ μέμψῃ ποτὲ τοὺς θεοὺς οὔτε
ἐγκαλέσεις ὡς ἀμελούμενος. ἄλλως δὲ οὐχ οἷόν
τε τοῦτο γίνεσθαι, ἐὰν μὴ ἄρῃς ἀπὸ τῶν οὐκ ἐφ᾽
ἡμῖν καὶ ἐν τοῖς ἐφ᾽ ἡμῖν μόνοις θῇς τὸ ἀγαθὸν καὶ
τὸ κακόν. ὡς, ἄν γέ τι ἐκείνων ὑπολάβῃς ἀγαθὸν

are being harmed. So make a habit of studying your social relationships – with neighbors, citizens, or army officers – and then you will discover the appropriate thing to do.

31. The essence of reverence concerning the gods is, first, to hold correct beliefs concerning their existence and their fine and just administration of the universe, and, second, to position yourself to obey them and accept whatever happens, complying with it willingly, on the understanding that what comes to pass has been ordained by their most excellent decision. In this way, you will never find fault with the gods, nor will you charge them with neglect. But such reverence is not possible unless you remove goodness and badness from the things not up to us and ascribe it only to the things that *are* up to us; for if you judge any of those other things to be good or bad, whenever you

ἢ κακόν, πᾶσα ἀνάγκη, ὅταν ἀποτυγχάνῃς ὧν
θέλεις καὶ περιπίπτῃς οἷς μὴ θέλεις, μέμψασθαί
σε καὶ μισεῖν τοὺς αἰτίους.

Πέφυκε γὰρ πρὸς τοῦτο πᾶν ζῷον τὰ μὲν
βλαβερὰ φαινόμενα καὶ τὰ αἴτια αὐτῶν φεύγειν
καὶ ἐκτρέπεσθαι, τὰ δὲ ὠφέλιμα καὶ τὰ αἴτια
αὐτῶν μετιέναι τε καὶ τεθηπέναι. ἀμήχανον οὖν
βλάπτεσθαί τινα οἰόμενον χαίρειν τῷ δοκοῦντι
βλάπτειν, ὥσπερ καὶ τὸ αὐτῇ τῇ βλάβῃ χαίρειν
ἀδύνατον. ἔνθεν καὶ πατὴρ ὑπὸ υἱοῦ λοιδορεῖται,
ὅταν τῶν δοκούντων ἀγαθῶν εἶναι τῷ παιδὶ μὴ
μεταδιδῷ· καὶ Πολυνείκην καὶ Ἐτεοκλέα τοῦτ'
ἐποίησε πολεμίους ἀλλήλοις τὸ ἀγαθὸν οἴεσθαι
τὴν τυραννίδα. διὰ τοῦτο καὶ ὁ γεωργὸς
λοιδορεῖ τοὺς θεούς, διὰ τοῦτο ὁ ναύτης, διὰ
τοῦτο ὁ ἔμπορος, διὰ τοῦτο οἱ τὰς γυναῖκας καὶ
τὰ τέκνα ἀπολλύντες. ὅπου γὰρ τὸ συμφέρον,
ἐκεῖ καὶ τὸ εὐσεβές. ὥστε, ὅστις ἐπιμελεῖται
τοῦ ὀρέγεσθαι ὡς δεῖ καὶ ἐκκλίνειν, ἐν τῷ
αὐτῷ καὶ εὐσεβείας ἐπιμελεῖται. σπένδειν δὲ καὶ

fail to get what you want and encounter what you don't want, you will be bound to blame the gods and hate them for being responsible.

It is every creature's nature, you see, to shun things that look harmful or cause harm, and to admire and pursue things that are beneficial or bring benefit. If you think you are being injured, you can no more enjoy what seems to be injuring you than you can enjoy the injury itself. Even fathers are maligned by their sons when they deprive them of things they think are good; and it was this, the belief that holding exclusive power is good, that created hostility between *Eteocles and Polyneices. For the same reason, farmers malign the gods, and sailors do so too, and merchants, and men who have lost their wives and children. Wherever people's interest lies, that's also the site of their reverence. If you are careful, then, to focus your desires and aversions where you should, you will be

θύειν καὶ ἀπάρχεσθαι κατὰ τὰ πάτρια +ἑκάστοις+
προσήκει καθαρῶς καὶ μὴ ἐπισεσυρμένως μηδὲ
ἀμελῶς μηδέ γε γλίσχρως μηδὲ ὑπὲρ δύναμιν.

32. Ὅταν μαντικῇ προσίῃς, μέμνησο, ὅτι,
τί μὲν ἀποβήσεται, οὐκ οἶδας, ἀλλὰ ἥκεις ὡς
παρὰ τοῦ μάντεως αὐτὸ πευσόμενος, ὁποῖον δέ
τι ἐστίν, ἐλήλυθας εἰδώς, εἴπερ εἶ φιλόσοφος.
εἰ γάρ ἐστί τι τῶν οὐκ ἐφ' ἡμῖν, πᾶσα ἀνάγκη
μήτε ἀγαθὸν αὐτὸ εἶναι μήτε κακόν. μὴ φέρε οὖν
πρὸς τὸν μάντιν ὄρεξιν ἢ ἔκκλισιν +(εἰ δὲ μὴ+
τρέμων αὐτῷ πρόσει), ἀλλὰ διεγνωκώς, ὅτι πᾶν
τὸ ἀποβησόμενον ἀδιάφορον καὶ οὐδὲν πρὸς σέ,
ὁποῖον δ' ἂν ᾖ, ἔσται αὐτῷ χρήσασθαι καλῶς καὶ
τοῦτο οὐδεὶς κωλύσει.

equally careful about reverence. Nevertheless, it is fitting for +everyone+ to perform religious rituals and make customary offerings as long as they act with a pure heart, not mechanically or carelessly, and not meanly or extravagantly.

32. Whenever you have your fortune taken, keep in mind that you don't know precisely what's going to happen (that's why you came to consult the fortune-teller), but if you are really a philosopher, you already know the sort of thing it is. For if it is one of the things not up to us, it must absolutely be neither good nor bad. So don't project your desire or aversion onto the fortune-teller +(otherwise you will come to him in great anxiety),+ but go in the understanding that every outcome is *indifferent—nothing that bears on you except as an opportunity, whatever it is like, to be put to excellent use and with no one to get in your way.

Θαρρῶν οὖν ὡς ἐπὶ συμβούλους ἔρχου τοὺς θεούς· καὶ λοιπόν, ὅταν τί σοι συμβουλευθῇ, μέμνησο τίνας συμβούλους παρέλαβες καὶ τίνων παρακούσεις ἀπειθήσας. ἔρχου δὲ ἐπὶ τὸ μαντεύεσθαι, καθάπερ ἠξίου Σωκράτης, ἐφ' ὧν ἡ πᾶσα σκέψις τὴν ἀναφορὰν εἰς τὴν ἔκβασιν ἔχει καὶ οὔτε ἐκ λόγου οὔτε ἐκ τέχνης τινὸς ἄλλης ἀφορμαὶ δίδονται πρὸς τὸ συνιδεῖν τὸ προκείμενον· ὥστε, ὅταν δεήσῃ συγκινδυνεῦσαι φίλῳ ἢ πατρίδι, μὴ μαντεύεσθαι, εἰ συγκινδυνευτέον. καὶ γὰρ ἂν προείπῃ σοι ὁ μάντις φαῦλα γεγονέναι τὰ ἱερά, δῆλον ὅτι θάνατος σημαίνεται ἢ πήρωσις μέρους τινὸς τοῦ σώματος ἢ φυγή· ἀλλ' αἱρεῖ ὁ λόγος καὶ σὺν τούτοις παρίστασθαι τῷ φίλῳ καὶ τῇ πατρίδι συγκινδυνεύειν. τοιγαροῦν τῷ μείζονι μάντει πρόσεχε, τῷ Πυθίῳ, ὃς ἐξέβαλε τοῦ ναοῦ τὸν οὐ βοηθήσαντα ἀναιρουμένῳ τῷ φίλῳ.

Go to the gods then, as your advisers, and go confidently. And next, when you have been given some advice, keep in mind whom you have taken as your advisers and whom you will be ignoring if you don't heed them. Proceed to fortune-telling in the way Socrates judged to be right for handling situations where the whole point of the inquiry is to learn what's going to happen, and where neither reason nor any other procedure can tell you what you are facing. And so, when there's a need for you to put yourself at risk on behalf of a friend or your country, those are not topics to consult a fortune-teller about. For even if the fortune-teller reports that the omens are inauspicious, what is clearly forecast is no more than death or bodily injury or exile. But reason requires that even under these circumstances you should support your friend and run risks for your country. So pay attention to the greater fortune-teller, *Pythian Apollo. He

33. Τάξον τινὰ ἤδη χαρακτῆρα σαυτῷ καὶ τύπον, ὃν φυλάξεις ἐπί τε σεαυτοῦ ὢν καὶ ἀνθρώποις ἐντυγχάνων.

Καὶ σιωπὴ τὸ πολὺ ἔστω ἢ λαλείσθω τὰ ἀναγκαῖα καὶ δι' ὀλίγων. σπανίως δέ ποτε καιροῦ παρακαλοῦντος ἐπὶ τὸ λέγειν λέξον μέν, ἀλλὰ περὶ οὐδενὸς τῶν τυχόντων· μὴ περὶ μονομαχιῶν, μὴ περὶ ἱπποδρομιῶν, μὴ περὶ ἀθλητῶν, μὴ περὶ βρωμάτων ἢ πομάτων, τῶν ἑκασταχοῦ, μάλιστα δὲ μὴ περὶ ἀνθρώπων ψέγων ἢ ἐπαινῶν ἢ συγκρίνων. ἂν μὲν οὖν οἷός τε ᾖς, μετάγαγε τοῖς σοῖς λόγοις καὶ τοὺς τῶν συνόντων ἐπὶ τὸ προσῆκον. εἰ δὲ ἐν ἀλλοφύλοις ἀποληφθεὶς τύχοις, σιώπα.

Γέλως μὴ πολὺς ἔστω μηδὲ ἐπὶ πολλοῖς μηδὲ ἀνειμένος.

threw out of the temple the man who gave no help to his friend when he was being killed.

33. Draw up right now a definite character and identity for yourself, one that you intend to stick to whether you are by yourself or in company.

Stay mainly silent or keep your conversation to the necessary minimum. On rare occasions, though, when the situation calls for it, engage in talk, but not about trite topics, like gladiators or horse races or athletes or food or drink—the things that come up all the time; and above all don't talk critically or flatteringly or judgmentally about people. By your own conversation, if you can, guide your friends' talk in a fitting direction, but if you find yourself all alone among strangers, stay silent.

Don't laugh much or often, and keep it down.

Ὅρκον παραίτησαι, εἰ μὲν οἷόν τε, εἰς ἅπαν, εἰ δὲ μή, ἐκ τῶν ἐνόντων.

Ἑστιάσεις τὰς ἔξω καὶ ἰδιωτικὰς διακρούου· ἐὰν δέ ποτε γίνηται καιρός, ἐντετάσθω σοι ἡ προσοχή, μήποτε ἄρα ὑπορρυῇς εἰς ἰδιωτισμόν. ἴσθι γάρ, ὅτι, ἐὰν ὁ ἑταῖρος ᾖ μεμολυσμένος, καὶ τὸν συνανατριβόμενον αὐτῷ συμμολύνεσθαι ἀνάγκη, κἂν αὐτὸς ὢν τύχῃ καθαρός.

Τὰ περὶ τὸ σῶμα μέχρι τῆς χρείας ψιλῆς παραλάμβανε, οἷον τροφάς, πόμα, ἀμπεχόνην, οἰκίαν, οἰκετίαν· τὸ δὲ πρὸς δόξαν ἢ τρυφὴν ἅπαν περίγραφε.

Περὶ ἀφροδίσια εἰς δύναμιν πρὸ γάμου καθαρευτέον· ἁπτομένῳ δὲ ὧν νομίμον ἐστι μεταληπτέον. μὴ μέντοι ἐπαχθὴς γίνου τοῖς χρωμένοις μηδὲ ἐλεγκτικός· μηδὲ πολλαχοῦ τὸ ὅτι αὐτὸς οὐ χρῇ, παράφερε.

Refuse completely to take an oath, or if that is out of the question, refuse to the extent that you can.

Excuse yourself from attending dinner parties given by *people outside your circle. But if you have to, be very careful not to slip into their ways. A companion's crudeness is bound to rub off on the one he is with, no matter how refined that person may be.

In things to do with the body—food, drink, clothes, housing, and servants—take only what you need, and cut out everything that is for show or luxury.

As for sex, abstain as far as possible before marriage, and if you do go in for it, do nothing that is socially unacceptable. But don't interfere with other people on account of their sex lives or criticize them, and don't broadcast your own abstinence.

Ἐάν τίς σοι ἀπαγγείλῃ ὅτι ὁ δεῖνά σε κακῶς
λέγει, μὴ ἀπολογοῦ πρὸς τὰ λεχθέντα, ἀλλ'
ἀποκρίνου διότι " ἠγνόει γὰρ τὰ ἄλλα τὰ
προσόντα μοι κακά, ἐπεὶ οὐκ ἂν ταῦτα μόνα
ἔλεγεν."

Εἰς τὰ θέατρα τὸ πολὺ παριέναι οὐκ ἀναγκαῖον.
εἰ δέ ποτε καιρὸς εἴη, μηδενὶ σπουδάζων φαίνου
ἢ σεαυτῷ, τοῦτ' ἔστι θέλε γίνεσθαι μόνα τὰ
γινόμενα καὶ νικᾶν μόνον τὸν νικῶντα· οὕτω γὰρ
οὐκ ἐμποδισθήσῃ. βοῆς δὲ καὶ τοῦ ἐπιγελᾶν
τινὶ ἢ ἐπὶ πολὺ συγκινεῖσθαι παντελῶς ἀπέχου.
καὶ μετὰ τὸ ἀπαλλαγῆναι μὴ πολλὰ περὶ τῶν
γεγενημένων διαλέγου, ὅσα μὴ φέρει πρὸς τὴν σὴν
ἐπανόρθωσιν· ἐμφαίνεται γὰρ ἐκ τοῦ τοιούτου, ὅτι
ἐθαύμασας τὴν θέαν.

Εἰς ἀκροάσεις τινῶν μὴ εἰκῆ μηδὲ ῥᾳδίως
πάριθι· παριὼν δὲ τὸ σεμνὸν καὶ τὸ εὐσταθὲς καὶ
ἅμα ἀνεπαχθὲς φύλασσε.

If you are told that someone is talking badly of you, don't defend yourself against the story but reply: "Obviously he didn't know my other faults, or he would have mentioned them as well."

There is no need for you to put in much of an appearance at the public games, but if the occasion arises don't let people see you supporting anyone's side except your own—I mean you should want the result to be exactly what it is and for the winner to be exactly the one who wins. In this way you won't be disappointed. Restrain yourself completely from shouting or laughing at anyone or getting strongly involved. After coming away, confine your account of the events to the experiences that bear on your own improvement. Otherwise people will think that you were impressed by the spectacle.

Don't show up casually or thoughtlessly at *public lectures, but when you do go behave

Ὅταν τινὶ μέλλῃς συμβαλεῖν, μάλιστα τῶν
ἐν ὑπεροχῇ δοκούντων, πρόβαλε σαυτῷ, τί ἂν
ἐποίησεν ἐν τούτῳ Σωκράτης ἢ Ζήνων, καὶ
οὐκ ἀπορήσεις τοῦ χρήσασθαι προσηκόντως
τῷ ἐμπεσόντι. ὅταν φοιτᾷς πρός τινα τῶν μέγα
δυναμένων, πρόβαλε, ὅτι οὐχ εὑρήσεις αὐτὸν
ἔνδον, ὅτι ἀποκλεισθήσῃ, ὅτι ἐντιναχθήσονταί
σοι αἱ θύραι, ὅτι οὐ φροντιεῖ σου. κἂν σὺν τούτοις
ἐλθεῖν καθήκῃ, ἐλθὼν φέρε τὰ γινόμενα καὶ
μηδέποτε εἴπῃς αὐτὸς πρὸς ἑαυτὸν ὅτι " οὐκ ἦν
τοσούτου "· ἰδιωτικὸν γὰρ καὶ διαβεβλημένον πρὸς
τὰ ἐκτός.

Ἐν ταῖς ὁμιλίαις ἀπέστω τὸ ἑαυτοῦ τινῶν ἔργων
ἢ κινδύνων ἐπὶ πολὺ καὶ ἀμέτρως μεμνῆσθαι.
οὐ γάρ, ὡς σοὶ ἡδύ ἐστι τὸ τῶν σῶν κινδύνων
μεμνῆσθαι, οὕτω καὶ τοῖς ἄλλοις ἡδύ ἐστι τὸ
τῶν σοὶ συμβεβηκότων ἀκούειν. ἀπέστω δὲ καὶ

decently and seriously and without causing offence.

Whenever you are going to meet anyone, especially someone thought to be important, ask yourself what Socrates or *Zeno would have done in this case, and then you will have no difficulty in handling the situation appropriately. And when you call on some high official, imagine that you will not find him at home, that you will be shut out, that the door will be slammed in your face, and that he will ignore you. But if, in spite of all this, you really have to go, accept it and go without ever telling yourself, "It was not worth all that." That's what an ordinary person would do, someone upset by mere circumstances.

In company don't go on at length about your own deeds or adventures. It may be pleasant for you to recount them, but others are less eager to hear about what has happened to

τὸ γέλωτα κινεῖν· ὀλισθηρὸς γὰρ ὁ τρόπος εἰς
ἰδιωτισμὸν καὶ ἅμα ἱκανὸς τὴν αἰδῶ τὴν πρὸς
σὲ τῶν πλησίον ἀνιέναι. ἐπισφαλὲς δὲ καὶ τὸ
εἰς αἰσχρολογίαν προελθεῖν. ὅταν οὖν τι συμβῇ
τοιοῦτον, ἂν μὲν εὔκαιρον ᾖ, καὶ ἐπίπληξον
τῷ προελθόντι· εἰ δὲ μή, τῷ γε ἀποσιωπῆσαι
καὶ ἐρυθριᾶσαι καὶ σκυθρωπάσαι δῆλος γίνου
δυσχεραίνων τῷ λόγῳ.

34. Ὅταν ἡδονῆς τινος φαντασίαν λάβῃς,
καθάπερ ἐπὶ τῶν ἄλλων, φύλασσε σαυτόν, μὴ
συναρπασθῇς ὑπ' αὐτῆς· ἀλλ' ἐκδεξάσθω σε τὸ
πρᾶγμα, καὶ ἀναβολήν τινα παρὰ σεαυτοῦ λάβε.
ἔπειτα μνήσθητι ἀμφοτέρων τῶν χρόνων, καθ' ὅν
τε ἀπολαύσεις τῆς ἡδονῆς, καὶ καθ' ὃν ἀπολαύσας
ὕστερον μετανοήσεις καὶ αὐτὸς σεαυτῷ
λοιδορήσῃ· καὶ τούτοις ἀντίθες ὅπως ἀποσχόμενος
χαιρήσεις καὶ ἐπαινέσεις αὐτὸς σεαυτόν. ἐὰν δέ
σοι καιρὸς φανῇ ἅψασθαι τοῦ ἔργου, πρόσεχε,

you. And don't try to be funny; it's behavior
that easily lapses into vulgarity, and it is also
liable to make your neighbors think less well
of you. Be warned, too, against encouraging
lewd conversation. If and when anything of the
sort happens, chide the person who has started
it if you can find the right moment, and if not,
show your dislike of the talk by staying silent,
blushing and frowning.

34. Whenever the impression of some pleasure comes into your mind, guard yourself
against being carried away by it, just as you
should do with impressions in general. Let the
thing wait a bit, and give yourself a pause. Then
think of both times—first the one when you
will enjoy the pleasure, and then the one after
that when you will be sorry and be angry with
yourself. Now contrast them with your joy and
self-satisfaction if you abstain. But if you find

μὴ ἡττήσῃ σε τὸ προσηνὲς αὐτοῦ καὶ ἡδὺ καὶ
ἐπαγωγόν· ἀλλ᾽ ἀντιτίθει, πόσῳ ἄμεινον τὸ
συνειδέναι σεαυτῷ ταύτην τὴν νίκην νενικηκότι.

35. Ὅταν τι διαγνούς, ὅτι ποιητέον ἐστί,
ποιῇς, μηδέποτε φύγῃς ὀφθῆναι πράσσων αὐτό,
κἂν ἀλλοῖόν τι μέλλωσιν οἱ πολλοὶ περὶ αὐτοῦ
ὑπολαμβάνειν. εἰ μὲν γὰρ οὐκ ὀρθῶς ποιεῖς,
αὐτὸ τὸ ἔργον φεῦγε· εἰ δὲ ὀρθῶς, τί φοβῇ τοὺς
ἐπιπλήξοντας οὐκ ὀρθῶς ;

36. Ὡς τὸ " ἡμέρα ἐστί " καὶ " νύξ ἐστι " πρὸς
μὲν τὸ διεζευγμένον μεγάλην ἔχει ἀξίαν, πρὸς δὲ
τὸ συμπεπλεγμένον ἀπαξίαν, οὕτω καὶ τὸ τὴν
μείζω μερίδα ἐκλέξασθαι πρὸς μὲν τὸ σῶμα ἐχέτω
ἀξίαν, πρὸς δὲ τὸ τὸ κοινωνικὸν ἐν ἑστιάσει, οἷον

this the right moment to embark on the affair, do beware that you are not being overwhelmed by its charm and sweetness and allure. Think how much better it is to realize that you have won this victory.

35. Whenever you do something you have decided ought to be done, never try to avoid being seen doing it, even if people in general may disapprove of it. If, of course, your action is wrong, just don't do it at all; but if it's right, why be afraid of people whose criticism is off the mark?

36. You can form a valid *disjunctive statement from the propositions "It is day" and "It is night" taken separately {"Either it is day, or it is night"}, but the *conjunctive statement {"Both it is day and it is night"} is completely invalid. Similarly, at a dinner party, choosing the larger share could have positive value for

δεῖ, φυλάξαι, ἀπαξίαν ἔχει. ὅταν οὖν συνεσθίῃς
ἑτέρῳ, μέμνησο, μὴ μόνον τὴν πρὸς τὸ σῶμα ἀξίαν
τῶν παρακειμένων ὁρᾶν, ἀλλὰ καὶ τὴν πρὸς τὸν
ἑστιάτορα αἰδῶ φυλάξαι.

37. Ἐὰν ὑπὲρ δύναμιν ἀναλάβῃς τι πρόσωπον,
καὶ ἐν τούτῳ ἠσχημόνησας καί, ὃ ἠδύνασο
ἐκπληρῶσαι, παρέλιπες.

38. Ἐν τῷ περιπατεῖν καθάπερ προσέχεις,
μὴ ἐπιβῇς ἥλῳ ἢ στρέψῃς τὸν πόδα σου, οὕτω
πρόσεχε, μὴ καὶ τὸ ἡγεμονικὸν βλάψῃς τὸ σεαυτοῦ.
καὶ τοῦτο ἐὰν ἐφ᾽ ἑκάστου ἔργου παραφυλάσσωμεν,
ἀσφαλέστερον ἁψόμεθα τοῦ ἔργου.

39. Μέτρον κτήσεως τὸ σῶμα ἑκάστῳ ὡς ὁ
ποὺς ὑποδήματος. ἐὰν μὲν οὖν ἐπὶ τούτου στῇς,

the body, but it has negative value for maintaining the sociability the occasion requires. So when you are dining with someone, be mindful not only to note the value of the dishes for your body but also to show respect for your host.

37. If you have taken on a *role beyond your capacity, you have demeaned yourself in it, and you have also passed up the role you could have filled creditably.

38. You are careful in walking not to step on a nail or twist your ankle, and you should be just as careful to do no harm to your commanding-faculty. If we stick to this rule in every action, we shall perform what we are doing more securely.

39. The body is the proper measure for each person's acquisitive needs, just as the foot is the

φυλάξεις τὸ μέτρον· ἐὰν δὲ ὑπερβῇς, ὡς κατὰ
κρημνοῦ λοιπὸν ἀνάγκη φέρεσθαι· καθάπερ καὶ
ἐπὶ τοῦ ὑποδήματος, ἐὰν ὑπὲρ τὸν πόδα ὑπερβῇς,
γίνεται κατάχρυσον ὑπόδημα, εἶτα πορφυροῦν,
κεντητόν. τοῦ γὰρ ἅπαξ ὑπὲρ τὸ μέτρον ὅρος
οὐθείς ἐστιν.

40. Αἱ γυναῖκες εὐθὺς ἀπὸ τεσσαρεσκαίδεκα
ἐτῶν ὑπὸ τῶν ἀνδρῶν κυρίαι καλοῦνται.
τοιγαροῦν ὁρῶσαι, ὅτι ἄλλο μὲν οὐδὲν αὐταῖς
πρόσεστι, μόνον δὲ συγκοιμῶνται τοῖς ἀνδράσι,
ἄρχονται καλλωπίζεσθαι καὶ ἐν τούτῳ πάσας
ἔχειν τὰς ἐλπίδας. προσέχειν οὖν ἄξιον, ἵνα
αἴσθωνται, διότι ἐπ᾽ οὐδενὶ ἄλλῳ τιμῶνται ἢ τῷ
κόσμιαι φαίνεσθαι καὶ αἰδήμονες.

41. Ἀφυΐας σημεῖον τὸ ἐνδιατρίβειν τοῖς περὶ
τὸ σῶμα, οἷον ἐπὶ πολὺ γυμνάζεσθαι, ἐπὶ πολὺ
ἐσθίειν, ἐπὶ πολὺ πίνειν, ἐπὶ πολὺ ἀποπατεῖν,

measure for a shoe. If you stick to this rule, you will keep the measure, but if you go beyond it, you are bound in the end to go over a cliff, so to speak. It's the same with the shoe if you exceed the foot; first comes a gilded shoe, and next one embroidered with purple. Once you exceed the measure, there is no limit.

40. As soon as they are fourteen, women are called "ladies" by men. So when they see that their only prospect is to go to bed with them, they begin to make themselves up and place all their hopes on their looks. They need to understand that the true basis for being respected is to appear refined and modest.

41. It is the mark of a crude disposition to spend most of one's time on bodily functions such as exercise, eating, drinking, defecating, and copulating. These are things to be done

ὀχεύειν. ἀλλὰ ταῦτα μὲν ἐν παρέργῳ ποιητέον· περὶ δὲ τὴν γνώμην ἡ πᾶσα ἔστω ἐπιστροφή.

42. Ὅταν σέ τις κακῶς ποιῇ ἢ κακῶς λέγῃ, μέμνησο, ὅτι καθήκειν αὐτῷ οἰόμενος ποιεῖ ἢ λέγει. οὐχ οἷόν τε οὖν ἀκολουθεῖν αὐτὸν τῷ σοὶ φαινομένῳ, ἀλλὰ τῷ ἑαυτῷ, ὥστε, εἰ κακῶς αὐτῷ φαίνεται, ἐκεῖνος βλάπτεται, ὅστις καὶ ἐξηπάτηται. καὶ γὰρ τὸ ἀληθὲς συμπεπλεγμένον ἄν τις ὑπολάβῃ ψεῦδος, οὐ τὸ συμπεπλεγμένον βέβλαπται, ἀλλ' ὁ ἐξαπατηθείς. ἀπὸ τούτων οὖν ὁρμώμενος πρᾴως ἕξεις πρὸς τὸν λοιδοροῦντα. ἐπιφθέγγου γὰρ ἐφ' ἑκάστῳ ὅτι " ἔδοξεν αὐτῷ."

43. Πᾶν πρᾶγμα δύο ἔχει λαβάς, τὴν μὲν φορητήν, τὴν δὲ ἀφόρητον. ὁ ἀδελφὸς ἐὰν ἀδικῇ, ἐντεῦθεν αὐτὸ μὴ λάμβανε, ὅτι ἀδικεῖ (αὕτη γὰρ

just incidentally. All your attention should be on your mind.

42. Whenever people treat you badly or criticize you, remember that they are only doing and saying what they think is appropriate for them. They cannot take their lead from *your* opinion but only from their own. So if their opinion is incorrect, they are the people who suffer harm because they are the ones who got it wrong. When someone takes a true *conjunctive statement to be false, no harm is done to the statement but only to the person making the mistake. If you start out from this position, you will be indulgent to your critics, and tell yourself each time, "That's what they thought."

43. Every situation has two handles, as it were, one making it supportable and the other insupportable. If your brother mistreats you,

ἡ λαβή ἐστιν αὐτοῦ οὐ φορητή), ἀλλὰ ἐκεῖθεν μᾶλλον, ὅτι ἀδελφός, ὅτι σύντροφος, καὶ λήψῃ αὐτὸ καθ' ὃ φορητόν.

44. Οὗτοι οἱ λόγοι ἀσύνακτοι· " ἐγώ σου πλουσιώτερός εἰμι, ἐγώ σου ἄρα κρείσσων "· "ἐγώ σου λογιώτερος, ἐγώ σου ἄρα κρείσσων " ἐκεῖνοι δὲ μᾶλλον συνακτικοί· " ἐγώ σου πλουσιώτερός εἰμι, ἡ ἐμὴ ἄρα κτῆσις τῆς σῆς κρείσσων"· "ἐγώ σου λογιώτερος, ἡ ἐμὴ ἄρα λέξις τῆς σῆς κρείσσων." σὺ δέ γε οὔτε κτῆσις εἶ οὔτε λέξις.

45. Λούεταί τις ταχέως· μὴ εἴπῃς ὅτι κακῶς, ἀλλ' ὅτι ταχέως. πίνει τις πολὺν οἶνον· μὴ εἴπῃς ὅτι κακῶς, ἀλλ' ὅτι πολυν. πρὶν γὰρ διαγνῶναι τὸ

don't fasten on the mistreatment—that is the insupportable handle of the situation—but on the other handle instead—that he is your brother, the boy you were raised with—and then you will fasten onto the situation in the way that makes it supportable.

44. These inferences are invalid: "I am richer than you, therefore I am better than you," and "I am more eloquent than you, therefore I am better than you." But the following inferences are more cogent: "I am richer than you, therefore my property is better than yours," or "I am more eloquent than you, therefore my diction is better than yours." But you yourself are neither property nor diction.

45. If people take a bath in a hurry, don't criticize them for their bathing, but say that they do it hurriedly. If they drink a lot of wine, don't

δόγμα, πόθεν οἶσθα, εἰ κακῶς ; οὕτως οὐ συμβήσεταί σοι ἄλλων μὲν φαντασίας καταληπτικὰς λαμβάνειν, ἄλλοις δὲ συγκατατίθεσθαι.

46. Μηδαμοῦ σεαυτὸν εἴπῃς φιλόσοφον μηδὲ λάλει τὸ πολὺ ἐν ἰδιώταις περὶ τῶν θεωρημάτων, ἀλλὰ ποίει τὸ ἀπὸ τῶν θεωρημάτων· οἷον ἐν συμποσίῳ μὴ λέγε, πῶς δεῖ ἐσθίειν, ἀλλ᾽ ἔσθιε, ὡς δεῖ. μέμνησο γάρ, ὅτι οὕτως ἀφῃρήκει πανταχόθεν Σωκράτης τὸ ἐπιδεικτικόν, ὥστε ἤρχοντο πρὸς αὐτὸν βουλόμενοι φιλοσόφοις ὑπ᾽ αὐτοῦ συσταθῆναι, κἀκεῖνος ἀπῆγεν αὐτούς. οὕτως ἠνείχετο παρορώμενος. κἂν περὶ θεωρήματός τινος ἐν ἰδιώταις ἐμπίπτῃ λόγος, σιώπα τὸ πολύ· μέγας γὰρ ὁ κίνδυνος εὐθὺς ἐξεμέσαι, ὃ οὐκ

criticize them for their drinking, but say that they drink a lot. Until you know their reasons, how do you know whether they acted wrongly. This way you will not combine *indubitable impressions of a situation with an *endorsement of something else that lacks this certainty.

46. Don't ever describe yourself as a philosopher or talk much among ordinary people about your philosophical principles; simply do what the principles prescribe. At a dinner party, for instance, don't discuss table manners, just eat nicely. Keep in mind that Socrates was so unostentatious that people came to him when they wanted him to introduce them to philosophers, and he took them along, so little did he mind being unacknowledged himself. If the conversation turns to a philosophical point, stay mainly silent, since there's a great risk that you will immediately spew up what you haven't

ἔπεψας. καὶ ὅταν εἴπῃ σοί τις, ὅτι οὐδὲν οἶσθα, καὶ σὺ μὴ δηχθῇς, τότε ἴσθι, ὅτι ἄρχῃ τοῦ ἔργου. ἐπεὶ καὶ τὰ πρόβατα οὐ χόρτον φέροντα τοῖς ποιμέσιν ἐπιδεικνύει πόσον ἔφαγεν, ἀλλὰ τὴν νομὴν ἔσω πέψαντα ἔρια ἔξω φέρει καὶ γάλα· καὶ σὺ τοίνυν μὴ τὰ θεωρήματα τοῖς ἰδιώταις ἐπιδείκνυε, ἀλλ' ἀπ' αὐτῶν πεφθέντων τὰ ἔργα.

47. Ὅταν εὐτελῶς ἡρμοσμένος ᾖς κατὰ τὸ σῶμα, μὴ καλλωπίζου ἐπὶ τούτῳ μηδ', ἂν ὕδωρ πίνῃς, ἐκ πάσης ἀφορμῆς λέγε, ὅτι ὕδωρ πίνεις. κἂν ἀσκῆσαί ποτε πρὸς πόνον θέλῃς, σεαυτῷ καὶ μὴ τοῖς ἔξω· μὴ τοὺς ἀνδριάντας περιλάμβανε·

fully absorbed. When your silence is taken for ignorance and you don't react, then believe me, you have made a real start on the philosophical enterprise. Sheep don't show how much they have eaten by bringing their fodder to the shepherds; they digest it inside their bodies, and on the outside produce wool and milk. Don't then, in your case, show off your philosophical principles to ordinary people, but show the actions that come from them once the principles have been absorbed.

47. When you have accustomed your body to a frugal regime, don't put on airs about it, and if you only drink water, don't broadcast the fact all the time. And if ever you want to go in for endurance training, do it for yourself and not for the world to see. Don't [be seen outside] *embracing statues. If you are very thirsty, you

ἀλλὰ διψῶν ποτὲ σφοδρῶς ἐπίσπασαι ψυχροῦ
ὕδατος καὶ ἔκπτυσον καὶ μηδενὶ εἴπῃς.

48. Ἰδιώτου στάσις καὶ χαρακτήρ· οὐδέποτε ἐξ
ἑαυτοῦ προσδοκᾷ ὠφέλειαν ἢ βλάβην, ἀλλ᾽ ἀπὸ
τῶν ἔξω. φιλοσόφου στάσις καὶ χαρακτήρ· πᾶσαν
ὠφέλειαν καὶ βλάβην ἐξ ἑαυτοῦ προσδοκᾷ.

Σημεῖα προκόπτοντος· οὐδένα ψέγει, οὐδένα
ἐπαινεῖ, οὐδένα μέμφεται, οὐδενὶ ἐγκαλεῖ, οὐδὲν
περὶ ἑαυτοῦ λέγει ὡς ὄντος τινὸς ἢ εἰδότος τι.
ὅταν ἐμποδισθῇ τι ἢ κωλυθῇ, ἑαυτῷ ἐγκαλεῖ.
κἄν τις αὐτὸν ἐπαινῇ, καταγελᾷ τοῦ ἐπαινοῦντος
αὐτὸς παρ᾽ ἑαυτῷ· κἄν ψέγῃ, οὐκ ἀπολογεῖται.
περίεισι δὲ καθάπερ οἱ ἄρρωστοι, εὐλαβούμενός
τι κινῆσαι τῶν καθισταμένων, πρὶν πῆξιν λαβεῖν.

can suck cold water and spit it out, but without telling anyone.

48. The stance and hallmark of ordinary persons is never looking for help or harm from themselves, but only from things that are on the outside. The stance and hallmark of philosophers is only looking for help and harm from themselves .

The signs of a person making progress are these: criticizing nobody, praising nobody, blaming nobody, accusing nobody, and saying nothing about oneself to indicate being someone or knowing something. Whenever such a person is frustrated or impeded, he accuses himself. If he's complimented, he laughs to himself at the one paying the compliment, and if he's criticized, he doesn't defend himself. He goes around like a patient, taking care not to injure any of his recovering limbs before they are

ὄρεξιν ἅπασαν ἦρκεν ἐξ ἑαυτοῦ· τὴν δ' ἔκκλισιν εἰς
μόνα τὰ παρὰ φύσιν τῶν ἐφ' ἡμῖν μετατέθεικεν.
ὁρμῇ πρὸς ἅπαντα ἀνειμένῃ χρῆται. ἂν ἠλίθιος
ἢ ἀμαθὴς δοκῇ, οὐ πεφρόντικεν. ἑνί τε λόγῳ, ὡς
ἐχθρὸν ἑαυτὸν παραφυλάσσει καὶ ἐπίβουλον.

49. Ὅταν τις ἐπὶ τῷ νοεῖν καὶ ἐξηγεῖσθαι
δύνασθαι τὰ Χρυσίππου βιβλία σεμνύνηται,
λέγε αὐτὸς πρὸς ἑαυτὸν ὅτι " εἰ μὴ Χρύσιππος
ἀσαφῶς ἐγεγράφει, οὐδὲν ἂν εἶχεν οὗτος, ἐφ' ᾧ
ἐσεμνύνετο." Ἐγὼ δὲ τί βούλομαι ; καταμαθεῖν
τὴν φύσιν καὶ ταύτῃ ἕπεσθαι. ζητῶ οὖν, τίς ἐστιν
ὁ ἐξηγούμενος· καὶ ἀκούσας, ὅτι Χρύσιππος,
ἔρχομαι πρὸς αὐτόν. ἀλλ' οὐ νοῶ τὰ γεγραμμένα·
ζητῶ οὖν τὸν ἐξηγούμενον. καὶ μέχρι τούτων οὔπω
σεμνὸν οὐδέν. ὅταν δὲ εὕρω τὸν ἐξηγούμενον,

fully firm. He has banished all desire, and he has transferred his aversion to the naturally disagreeable things that are up to us. He is relaxed in all his motivations. He doesn't care if he appears simple-minded or ignorant. In a word, he keeps watch on himself as though he were his own enemy plotting an attack.

49. Whenever people take pride in their ability to understand and explain *Chrysippus's books, say to yourself: "If Chrysippus had not written obscurely, they would have nothing to be proud of." What do I want then for myself? I want to understand nature and follow its lead. So I look for someone to interpret nature for me, and on hearing that Chrysippus can do that I go to him. But I don't understand his writings, so I look for an interpreter of *them*. Thus far there is nothing for me to take pride in. After I have found the interpreter, I still have to

ἀπολείπεται χρῆσθαι τοῖς παρηγγελμένοις· τοῦτο
αὐτὸ μόνον σεμνόν ἐστιν. ἂν δὲ αὐτὸ τοῦτο τὸ
ἐξηγεῖσθαι θαυμάσω, τί ἄλλο ἢ γραμματικὸς
ἀπετελέσθην ἀντὶ φιλοσόφου; πλήν γε δὴ ὅτι ἀντὶ
Ὁμήρου Χρύσιππον ἐξηγούμενος. μᾶλλον οὖν,
ὅταν τις εἴπῃ μοι " ἐπανάγνωθί μοι Χρύσιππον,"
ἐρυθριῶ, ὅταν μὴ δύνωμαι ὅμοια τὰ ἔργα καὶ
σύμφωνα ἐπιδεικνύειν τοῖς λόγοις.

50. Ὅσα προτίθεται, τούτοις ὡς νόμοις, ὡς
ἀσεβήσων, ἂν παραβῇς, ἔμμενε. ὅ τι δ᾽ ἂν ἐρῇ
τις περὶ σοῦ, μὴ ἐπιστρέφου· τοῦτο γὰρ οὐκ ἔτ᾽
ἐστὶ σόν.

51. Εἰς ποῖον ἔτι χρόνον ἀναβάλλῃ τὸ τῶν
βελτίστων ἀξιοῦν σεαυτὸν καὶ ἐν μηδενὶ
παραβαίνειν τὸν διαιροῦντα λόγον; παρείληφας
τὰ θεωρήματα, οἷς ἔδει σε συμβάλλειν, καὶ
συμβέβληκας. ποῖον οὖν ἔτι διδάσκαλον

put the precepts into practice—that's the only thing to be proud of. But if what impresses me is just the interpreting itself, I have ended up as a literary scholar and not a philosopher, except that I am interpreting Chrysippus instead of Homer. Rather than showing pride, therefore, when I am asked to expound Chrysippus, I blush at my inability to exhibit the sort of actions that would match his statements.

50. In all your projects, keep to them as laws that it would be totally wrong to transgress. And as to anything that people may say about you, ignore it because it doesn't belong to you.

51. How long will you delay thinking yourself worthy of the best and making reason your decisive principle in everything? You have received the principles you ought to endorse, and you have endorsed them. What sort of

προσδοκᾷς, ἵνα εἰς ἐκεῖνον ὑπερθῇ τὴν
ἐπανόρθωσιν ποιῆσαι τὴν σεαυτοῦ ; οὐκ ἔτι
εἶ μειράκιον, ἀλλὰ ἀνὴρ ἤδη τέλειος. ἂν νῦν
ἀμελήσῃς καὶ ῥαθυμήσῃς καὶ ἀεὶ προθέσεις ἐκ
προθέσεως ποιῇ καὶ ἡμέρας ἄλλας ἐπ' ἄλλαις
ὁρίζῃς, μεθ' ἃς προσέξεις σεαυτῷ, λήσεις σεαυτὸν
οὐ προκόψας, ἀλλ' ἰδιώτης διατελέσεις καὶ ζῶν καὶ
ἀποθνῄσκων. ἤδη οὖν ἀξίωσον σεαυτὸν βιοῦν ὡς
τέλειον καὶ προκόπτοντα· καὶ πᾶν τὸ βέλτιστον
φαινόμενον ἔστω σοι νόμος ἀπαράβατος.
κἂν ἐπίπονόν τι ᾖ ἢ ἡδὺ ἢ ἔνδοξον ἢ ἄδοξον
προσάγηται, μέμνησο, ὅτι νῦν ὁ ἀγὼν καὶ ἤδη
πάρεστι τὰ Ὀλύμπια καὶ οὐκ ἔστιν ἀναβάλλεσθαι
οὐκέτι καὶ ὅτι παρὰ μίαν ἡμέραν καὶ ἓν
πρᾶγμα καὶ ἀπόλλυται προκοπὴ καὶ σῴζεται.
Σωκράτης οὕτως ἀπετελέσθη, ἐπὶ πάντων τῶν
προσαγομένων αὐτῷ μηδενὶ ἄλλῳ προσέχων ἢ
τῷ λόγῳ. σὺ δὲ εἰ καὶ μήπω εἶ Σωκράτης, ὡς
Σωκράτης γε εἶναι βουλόμενος ὀφείλεις βιοῦν.

teacher, then, are you still waiting for, so that you can transfer the correction of yourself to him? You are not a boy anymore, but already a full-grown man. If you are negligent now and lazy and always procrastinating, and settling on the day after tomorrow and the next as when you will take yourself in hand, you will fail to see that you are making no progress but spending your entire life as an ordinary person until you die. Right now, then, think yourself worthy to live as a grown-up making progress; and take your view of the best to be the rule that you never transgress. And whatever you encounter that is painful or pleasant or popular or unpopular, keep in mind that *now* is the contest, and here right now are the Olympic games, and that postponement is no longer an option, and that your progress is saved or ruined by a single day and a single action. That's how Socrates perfected himself, by attending

52. Ὁ πρῶτος καὶ ἀναγκαιότατος τόπος ἐστὶν
ἐν φιλοσοφίᾳ ὁ τῆς χρήσεως τῶν θεωρημάτων, οἷον
τὸ μὴ ψεύδεσθαι· ὁ δεύτερος ὁ τῶν ἀποδείξεων,
οἷον πόθεν ὅτι οὐ δεῖ ψεύδεσθαι ; τρίτος ὁ αὐτῶν
τούτων βεβαιωτικὸς καὶ διαρθρωτικός, οἷον πόθεν
ὅτι τοῦτο ἀπόδειξις ; τί γάρ ἐστιν ἀπόδειξις, τί
ἀκολουθία, τί μάχη, τί ἀληθές, τί ψεῦδος ; οὐκοῦν ὁ
μὲν τρίτος τόπος ἀναγκαῖος διὰ τὸν δεύτερον, ὁ δὲ
δεύτερος διὰ τὸν πρῶτον· ὁ δὲ ἀναγκαιότατος καὶ
ὅπου ἀναπαύεσθαι δεῖ, ὁ πρῶτος. ἡμεῖς δὲ ἔμπαλιν
ποιοῦμεν· ἐν γὰρ τῷ τρίτῳ τόπῳ διατρίβομεν
καὶ περὶ ἐκεῖνόν ἐστιν ἡμῖν ἡ πᾶσα σπουδή· τοῦ
δὲ πρώτου παντελῶς ἀμελοῦμεν. τοιγαροῦν

to nothing except reason in everything he encountered. You yourself too, even though you are not yet Socrates, ought to live as someone who wants to be a Socrates.

52. The first and most necessary area of philosophy is application of the principles, such as not to lie. The second area treats their proofs, such as the grounds for the principle that one should not lie. Third comes the field that confirms and analyzes the proofs, such as investigating what makes this a proof, what proof is as such, and what validity, contradiction, truth and falsehood are. Therefore, the third area is necessary because of the second, and the second because of the first, but it is the first that is the most necessary and the one where we ought to stay. In fact, though, we do the opposite. We spend our time on the third area, concentrating all our enthusiasm on it and neglecting the first

ψευδόμεθα μέν, πῶς δὲ ἀποδείκνυται ὅτι οὐ δεῖ
ψεύδεσθαι, πρόχειρον ἔχομεν.

53. Ἐπὶ παντὸς πρόχειρα ἑκτέον ταῦτα·

Ἄγου δέ μ᾽, ὦ Ζεῦ, καὶ σύ γ᾽ ἡ Πεπρωμένη,
ὅποι ποθ᾽ ὑμῖν εἰμὶ διατεταγμένος·
ὡς ἕψομαί γ᾽ ἄοκνος· ἢν δέ γε μὴ θέλω,
κακὸς γενόμενος, οὐδὲν ἧττον ἕψομαι.

" Ὅστις δ᾽ ἀνάγκῃ συγκεχώρηκεν καλῶς, σοφὸς
    παρ᾽ ἡμῖν, καὶ τὰ θεῖ᾽ ἐπίσταται."

" Ἀλλ᾽, ὦ Κρίτων, εἰ ταύτῃ τοῖς θεοῖς φίλον, ταύτῃ
    γενέσθω."

" Ἐμὲ δὲ Ἄνυτος καὶ Μέλητος ἀποκτεῖναι μὲν
    δύνανται, βλάψαι δὲ οὔ."

one completely. The result is that we do tell lies, while we are ready to advance the proofs that we shouldn't.

53. On every occasion we should have the following *quotations to hand:

Lead me, O Zeus, and you, O Destiny,
Wherever you have ordained for me.
I will follow unflinching. But if, grown bad,
I should refuse, I will follow none the less.

Whosoever complies nobly with necessity
We count as wise and knowing things divine.

Well, Crito, if it [my death] is pleasing to the
    gods, so let it be.

Anytus and Meletus [Socrates' Athenian prosecu-
    tors] can kill me, but they cannot harm me.

From the *Discourses*

This part of the current work is a translation of nine excerpts from three of the four extant books of Epictetus's *Discourses*. These books in total comprise almost one hundred items ranging in length from about twenty pages of a modern volume to less than a single page. The longest item, from which I have taken the passages numbered 3 and 4, is entitled simply *On Freedom*. Arrian or a later editor applied this title. Apt though it is, the topic of freedom is ubiquitous throughout the *Discourses* just as it is in the *Encheiridion*. I have supplied the titles to each of these excerpts, to indicate Epictetus's multipronged treatment of his favorite theme.

In making this selection, I have had two principal goals: first, to supplement the *Encheiridion* with additional philosophical content, and second

to give readers a taste of Epictetus's dialogical style. To savor Epictetus in depth, the *Discourses* are indispensable, but Arrian did an equally fine job in extracting from them the compendious guidance of the *Encheiridion*. As the little classic that it is, you can take it everywhere, and if you are like me, you will find its abrasive message provocative, invigorating, and even comforting.

1.12.8–23

ὁ δὲ παιδευόμενος ταύτην ὀφείλει τὴν ἐπιβολὴν
ἔχων ἐλθεῖν ἐπὶ τὸ παιδεύεσθαι, "πῶς ἂν ἑποίμην
ἐγὼ ἐν παντὶ τοῖς θεοῖς καὶ πῶς ἂν εὐαρεστοίην τῇ
θείᾳ διοικήσει καὶ πῶς ἂν γενοίμην ἐλεύθερος;"
ἐλεύθερος γάρ ἐστιν, ᾧ γίνεται πάντα κατὰ
προαίρεσιν καὶ ὃν οὐδεὶς δύναται κωλῦσαι. τί οὖν;
ἀπόνοιά ἐστιν ἡ ἐλευθερία; μὴ γένοιτο. μανία γὰρ
καὶ ἐλευθερία εἰς ταὐτὸν οὐκ ἔρχεται. "ἀλλ᾽ ἐγὼ
θέλω πᾶν τὸ δοκοῦν μοι ἀποβαίνειν, κἂν ὁπωσοῦν
δοκῇ." μαινόμενος εἶ, παραφρονεῖς. οὐκ οἶδας,
ὅτι καλόν τι ἐλευθερία ἐστὶ καὶ ἀξιόλογον; τὸ δ᾽
ὡς ἔτυχέν με βούλεσθαι τὰ ὡς ἔτυχεν δόξαντα

1 Learning to Desire Each Thing as It Happens

The person who is getting an education ought to approach this process with the following aim:

How can I follow the gods in everything, how can I be content with the divine administration, and how can I become free?

Well, you are free if nothing happens that conflicts with your will and if no one is able to obstruct you.

What does that mean? Are you telling me that freedom is madness?

No, of course not. Freedom and madness don't go together.

But I want my every wish to come to pass, however crazy that may seem.

You really are mad, you are raving. Don't you know that *freedom is something fine and wonderful? To be so happy-go-lucky in one's

γίνεσθαι, τοῦτο κινδυνεύει οὐ μόνον οὐκ εἶναι καλόν, ἀλλὰ καὶ πάντων αἴσχιστον εἶναι. πῶς γὰρ ἐπὶ γραμματικῶν ποιοῦμεν; βούλομαι γράφειν ὡς θέλω τὸ Δίωνος ὄνομα; οὔ· ἀλλὰ διδάσκομαι θέλειν, ὡς δεῖ γράφεσθαι. τί ἐπὶ μουσικῶν; ὡσαύτως. τί ἐν τῷ καθόλου, ὅπου τέχνη τις ἢ ἐπιστήμη ἐστίν; εἰ δὲ μή, οὐδενὸς ἦν ἄξιον τὸ ἐπίστασθαί τι, εἰ ταῖς ἑκάστων βουλήσεσι προσηρμόζετο. ἐνταῦθα οὖν μόνον ἐπὶ τοῦ μεγίστου καὶ κυριωτάτου, τῆς ἐλευθερίας, ὡς ἔτυχεν ἐφεῖταί μοι θέλειν; οὐδαμῶς, ἀλλὰ τὸ παιδεύεσθαι τοῦτ' ἔστι μανθάνειν ἕκαστα οὕτω θέλειν ὡς γίνεται. πῶς δὲ γίνεται; ὡς διέταξεν αὐτὰ ὁ διατάσσων. διέταξε δὲ θέρος εἶναι καὶ

wishes as to want every whim fulfilled is tantamount to being the reverse of fine—utterly shameful in fact. Think how we proceed in the case of the alphabet. Do I want to write the name "Dio" in whatever way I like? No, I am taught to like it the way it should be written. How is it in music? Just the same, and so it is quite generally wherever some skill or expertise is involved. Otherwise, if knowledge were adjusted to everyone's individual whims, there would be no point in learning anything.

Is it only here, then, in the case of the greatest and most important thing, freedom, that I am allowed to be happy-go-lucky in my wishes?

Not here, least of all! Because education is precisely learning to want all individual things to happen just as they do happen. And how do they happen? In the way that the one who has arranged them has arranged. He has arranged

χειμῶνα καὶ φορὰν καὶ ἀφορίαν καὶ ἀρετὴν καὶ
κακίαν καὶ πάσας τὰς τοιαύτας ἐναντιότητας
ὑπὲρ συμφωνίας τῶν ὅλων ἡμῶν θ᾽ ἑκάστῳ σῶμα
καὶ μέρη τοῦ σώματος καὶ κτῆσιν καὶ κοινωνοὺς
ἔδωκεν.

Ταύτης οὖν τῆς διατάξεως μεμνημένους
ἔρχεσθαι δεῖ ἐπὶ τὸ παιδεύεσθαι, οὐχ ἵν᾽
ἀλλάξωμεν τὰς ὑποθέσεις (οὔτε γὰρ δίδοται ἡμῖν
οὔτ᾽ ἄμεινον), ἀλλ᾽ ἵνα οὕτως ἐχόντων τῶν περὶ
ἡμᾶς ὡς ἔχει καὶ πέφυκεν αὐτοὶ τὴν γνώμην τὴν
αὐτῶν συνηρμοσμένην τοῖς γινομένοις ἔχωμεν. τί
γάρ; ἐνδέχεται φυγεῖν ἀνθρώπους; καὶ πῶς οἷόν
τε; ἀλλὰ συνόντας αὐτοῖς ἐκείνους ἀλλάξαι; καὶ τίς
ἡμῖν δίδωσιν; τί οὖν ἀπολείπεται ἢ τίς εὑρίσκεται
μηχανὴ πρὸς τὴν χρῆσιν αὐτῶν; τοιαύτη, δι᾽
ἧς ἐκεῖνοι μὲν ποιήσουσι τὰ φαινόμενα αὐτοῖς,

for there to be summer and winter, plenty and dearth, virtue and vice, and all such opposites on behalf of the harmony of the universe. And he has given each of us a body and bodily parts and property and fellow human beings.

Mindful thereafter of this arrangement, we should proceed to education not in order to change the conditions (for this is not granted to us nor would it be better) but in order that, with things about us as they are and as their nature is, we may keep our minds in harmony with what happens. Tell me then.

Is it possible to escape from people?

How could that happen?

But is it possible to change them by being in their company?

Who gives us that option?

What else is there, then, and what resource can we find for dealing with them?

ἡμεῖς δ' οὐδὲν ἧττον κατὰ φύσιν ἕξομεν. σὺ δ'
ἀταλαίπωρος εἶ καὶ δυσάρεστος κἂν μὲν μόνος
ἦς, ἐρημίαν καλεῖς τοῦτο, ἂν δὲ μετὰ ἀνθρώπων,
ἐπιβούλους λέγεις καὶ λῃστάς, μέμφῃ δὲ καὶ
γονεῖς τοὺς σεαυτοῦ καὶ τέκνα καὶ ἀδελφοὺς
καὶ γείτονας. ἔδει δὲ μόνον μένοντα ἡσυχίαν
καλεῖν αὐτὸ καὶ ἐλευθερίαν καὶ ὅμοιον τοῖς θεοῖς
ἡγεῖσθαι αὐτόν, μετὰ πολλῶν δ' ὄντα μὴ ὄχλον
καλεῖν μηδὲ θόρυβον μηδ' ἀηδίαν, ἀλλ' ἑορτὴν
καὶ πανήγυριν καὶ οὕτως πάντα εὐαρέστως
δέχεσθαι.

   Τίς οὖν ἡ κόλασις τοῖς οὐ προσδεχομένοις;
τὸ οὕτως ἔχειν ὡς ἔχουσιν. δυσαρεστεῖ τις τῷ
μόνος εἶναι; ἔστω ἐν ἐρημίᾳ. δυσαρεστεῖ τις
τοῖς γονεῦσιν; ἔστω κακὸς υἱὸς καὶ πενθείτω.
δυσαρεστεῖ τοῖς τέκνοις; ἔστω κακὸς πατήρ.
"βάλε αὐτὸν εἰς φυλακήν." ποίαν φυλακήν; ὅπου
νῦν ἐστιν. ἄκων γάρ ἐστιν· ὅπου δέ τις ἄκων
ἐστίν, ἐκεῖνο φυλακὴ αὐτῷ ἐστιν. καθὸ καὶ
Σωκράτης οὐκ ἦν ἐν φυλακῇ, ἑκὼν γὰρ ἦν.

The sort of resource, whereby they will do what seems good to them, but we shall just as surely be in harmony with nature. Yet you are unhappy and discontented. If you are alone, you call it isolation, but if you are in company, you call people schemers and robbers. You even find fault with your parents and children and brothers and neighbors. But when you are alone, you should call it peace and freedom and liken yourself to the gods. And when you are in a group, you should not call it a crowd and a mob and an unpleasantness, but a party and a festival, and so accept everything cheerfully.

What, then, is the punishment for those who don't accept?

To be just as they are.

A man doesn't like being alone.

Let him be in isolation.

He doesn't like his parents.

Let him be a bad son and moan.

FROM THE *DISCOURSES*

2.1.21–4

Τίς οὖν τούτων τῶν δογμάτων καρπός; ὅνπερ
δεῖ κάλλιστόν τ᾽ εἶναι καὶ πρεπωδέστατον
τοῖς τῷ ὄντι παιδευομένοις, ἀταραξία ἀφοβία
ἐλευθερία. οὐ γὰρ τοῖς πολλοῖς περὶ τούτων
πιστευτέον, οἳ λέγουσιν μόνοις ἐξεῖναι
παιδεύεσθαι τοῖς ἐλευθέροις, ἀλλὰ τοῖς
φιλοσόφοις μᾶλλον, οἳ λέγουσι μόνους τοὺς
παιδευθέντας ἐλευθέρους εἶναι.—Πῶς τοῦτο;—
Οὕτως· νῦν ἄλλο τί ἐστιν ἐλευθερία ἢ τὸ ἐξεῖναι

He doesn't like his children.
Let him be a bad father.
Throw him in jail!
What jail? You mean where he is now. For he is there against his will, and wherever someone is against his will, there he is in jail. That's how Socrates was not in jail because he was there willingly.

2 Freedom from Emotional Distress

What is the fruit of these [Stoic] doctrines?
The very thing that has to be the finest and most fitting outcome for people who are getting a real education—tranquility, fearlessness, and freedom. For on these matters we should not trust the many people who say that education is only available to the free, but rather the philosophers who say that only the educated are free.

ὡς βουλόμεθα διεξάγειν; "οὐδέν." λέγετε δή
μοι, ὦ ἄνθρωποι, βούλεσθε ζῆν ἁμαρτάνοντες;
"οὐ βουλόμεθα." οὐδεὶς τοίνυν ἁμαρτάνων
ἐλεύθερός ἐστιν. βούλεσθε ζῆν φοβούμενοι,
βούλεσθε λυπούμενοι, βούλεσθε ταρασσόμενοι;
"οὐδαμῶς." οὐδεὶς ἄρα οὔτε φοβούμενος οὔτε
λυπούμενος οὔτε ταρασσόμενος ἐλεύθερός
ἐστιν, ὅστις δ᾽ ἀπήλλακται λυπῶν καὶ φόβων καὶ
ταραχῶν, οὗτος τῇ αὐτῇ ὁδῷ καὶ τοῦ δουλεύειν
ἀπήλλακται.

4.1.54–60

Δοκεῖ σοι μέγα τι εἶναι καὶ γενναῖον ἡ ἐλευθερία
καὶ ἀξιόλογον ;—Πῶς γὰρ οὔ ;—Ἔστιν οὖν

What do you mean by this?

Well, ask yourself about freedom in this time of ours; doesn't it consist simply in the power to live as we wish?

Absolutely.

Tell me then, you people, do you wish to live in error?

We do not.

That's right; no one is free who is in error. Do you wish to live in fear and sorrow and disturbance?

Certainly not.

So, no one who is fearful or sorrowful or disturbed is free, but the person who is relieved of sorrows and fears and disturbances is relieved of enslavement by the very same process.

3 Freedom from Subservience

Do you think freedom is something great and noble and valuable?

τυγχάνοντά τινος οὕτως μεγάλου καὶ ἀξιολόγου
καὶ γενναίου ταπεινὸν εἶναι ;—Οὐκ ἔστιν.—Ὅταν
οὖν ἴδῃς τινὰ ὑποπεπτωκότα ἑτέρῳ ἢ κολακεύοντα
παρὰ τὸ φαινόμενον αὐτῷ, λέγε καὶ τοῦτον θαρρῶν
μὴ εἶναι ἐλεύθερον· καὶ μὴ μόνον, ἂν δειπναρίου
ἕνεκα αὐτὸ ποιῇ, ἀλλὰ κἂν ἐπαρχίας ἕνεκα κἂν
ὑπατείας. ἀλλ᾽ ἐκείνους μὲν μικροδούλους λέγε
τοὺς μικρῶν τινῶν ἕνεκα ταῦτα ποιοῦντας, τούτους
δ᾽, ὡς εἰσὶν ἄξιοι, μεγαλοδούλους.—Ἔστω καὶ
ταῦτα.—Δοκεῖ δέ σοι ἡ ἐλευθερία αὐτεξούσιόν τι
εἶναι καὶ αὐτόνομον ;—Πῶς γὰρ οὔ ;—Ὅντινα
οὖν ἐπ᾽ ἄλλῳ κωλῦσαι ἔστι καὶ ἀναγκάσαι, θαρρῶν
λέγε μὴ εἶναι ἐλεύθερον. καὶ μή μοι πάππους

Of course.

Is it possible to be submissive if you obtain such a great and valuable and noble thing?

It is not.

So whenever you see someone groveling to another person or flattering him insincerely, you can confidently say that this man also is not free, and not only if he is doing it for the sake of a meager meal but even if he is hoping for a governorship or a consulship. Call people who act like this for small things petty slaves, and call the others, as they deserve, slaves on the grand scale.

You are right again.

Do you think freedom is something in one's own power and self-determined?

Of course.

You can confidently say, then, that no man is free if someone else has the power to obstruct and compel him. And don't consider his

αὐτοῦ καὶ προπάππους βλέπε καὶ ὠνὴν ζήτει καὶ
πρᾶσιν, ἀλλ' ἂν ἀκούσῃς λέγοντος ἔσωθεν καὶ ἐκ
πάθους "κύριε," κἂν δώδεκα ῥάβδοι προάγωσιν,
λέγε δοῦλον· κἂν ἀκούσῃς λέγοντος "τάλας ἐγώ,
οἷα πάσχω," λέγε δοῦλον· ἂν ἁπλῶς ἀποκλαιόμενον
ἴδῃς, μεμφόμενον, δυσροοῦντα, λέγε δοῦλον
περιπόρφυρον ἔχοντα. ἂν οὖν μηδὲν τούτων ποιῇ,
μήπω εἴπῃς ἐλεύθερον, ἀλλὰ τὰ δόγματα αὐτοῦ
κατάμαθε, μή τι ἀναγκαστά, μή τι κωλυτικά, μή
τι δυσροητικά· κἂν εὕρῃς τοιοῦτον, λέγε δοῦλον
ἀνοχὰς ἔχοντα ἐν Σατουρναλίοις· λέγε, ὅτι ὁ κύριος
αὐτοῦ ἀποδημεῖ· εἶθ' ἥξει καὶ γνώσῃ οἷα πάσχει.
—Τίς ἥξει ;—Πᾶς ὃς ἂν ἐξουσίαν ἔχῃ τῶν ὑπ'
αὐτοῦ τινὸς θελομένων πρὸς τὸ περιποιῆσαι
ταῦτα ἢ ἀφελέσθαι.—Οὕτως οὖν πολλοὺς

family tree, or investigate whether he was ever bought or sold, but if you hear him say, "Yes sir," within himself and with feeling, call him a slave even if he is preceded by a consular retinue. And if you hear him say, "Poor me, what things I suffer," call him a slave. In short, if you see him wailing, complaining, and unhappy, call him a slave in official dress. If, however, he does none of these things, don't call him free yet but examine his judgments to see whether they are in any way subject to compulsion or obstruction or unhappiness, and if you find him to be of that sort, call him a slave on vacation at the *Saturnalia, and say that his master is away. Soon he will come back, and then you will learn the nature of this man's sufferings.

Who will come back?

Everyone who has authority over anything that the man wants, either to get it for him or to take it away from him.

κυρίους ἔχομεν ;—Οὕτως. τὰ γὰρ πράγματα
προτέρους τούτων κυρίους ἔχομεν· ἐκεῖνα δὲ
πολλά ἐστιν. διὰ ταῦτα ἀνάγκη καὶ τοὺς τούτων
τινὸς ἔχοντας ἐξουσίαν κυρίους εἶναι· ἐπεί τοι
οὐδεὶς αὐτὸν τὸν Καίσαρα φοβεῖται, ἀλλὰ θάνατον,
φυγήν, ἀφαίρεσιν τῶν ὄντων, φυλακήν, ἀτιμίαν.
οὐδὲ φιλεῖ τις τὸν Καίσαρα, ἂν μή τι ᾖ πολλοῦ
ἄξιος, ἀλλὰ πλοῦτον φιλοῦμεν, δημαρχίαν,
στρατηγίαν, ὑπατείαν. ὅταν ταῦτα φιλῶμεν καὶ
μισῶμεν καὶ φοβώμεθα, ἀνάγκη τοὺς ἐξουσίαν
αὐτῶν ἔχοντας κυρίους ἡμῶν εἶναι.

4.1.64–80

Τὸν ἐφιέμενόν τινος τῶν ἐπ' ἄλλοις ὄντων
ἐνδέχεται ἀκώλυτον εἶναι ;—Οὔ.—Ἐνδέχεται
ἀπαραπόδιστον ;—Οὔ.—Οὐκοῦν οὐδ' ἐλεύθερον.

Do we have so many masters then?

Oh yes! Prior to people we have masters in the form of circumstances, and there are lots of those. For this reason, then, everyone with authority over any of our circumstances is bound to be our master. Caesar himself, you see, is not what people fear; they fear death, exile, confiscation of property, prison, loss of citizenship. In the same way, no one loves Caesar himself, unless he happens to be an outstanding person; what we love are wealth and high position in government or military service. Whenever these are the things that we love and hate and fear, it must be the case that those who have authority over them are our masters.

4 Freedom to Assent without Impediment

Is it possible for someone who desires any of the things that are up to others to be unimpeded?

It is not.

ὅρα οὖν· πότερον οὐδὲν ἔχομεν, ὃ ἐφ' ἡμῖν μόνοις
ἐστίν, ἢ πάντα, ἢ τὰ μὲν ἐφ' ἡμῖν ἐστίν, τὰ δ' ἐπ'
ἄλλοις ;—Πῶς λέγεις;—Τὸ σῶμα ὅταν θέλῃς
ὁλόκληρον εἶναι, ἐπὶ σοί ἐστιν ἢ οὔ ;—Οὐκ ἐπ'
ἐμοί.—Ὅταν δ' ὑγιαίνειν ;—Οὐδὲ τοῦτο.—
Ὅταν δὲ καλὸν εἶναι ;—Οὐδὲ τοῦτο.—Ζῆν
δὲ καὶ ἀποθανεῖν ;—Οὐδὲ τοῦτο.—Οὐκοῦν
τὸ μὲν σῶμα ἀλλότριον, ὑπεύθυνον παντὸς τοῦ
ἰσχυροτέρου.—Ἔστω.—Τὸν ἀγρὸν δ' ἐπὶ σοί

Is it possible for them to be unconstrained?

It is not.

Therefore they cannot be free, either. So think: do we have nothing that is exclusively up to us, or is everything like that, or are some things up to us and some things up to others?

How do you mean?

When you want your body to be completely sound, is it up to you, or is it not?

It is not up to me.

And when you want it to be in good health?

Not that either.

And when you want it to be handsome?

No again.

And when you want to live or to die?

Not that either.

Therefore, your body is not your own property. It is dependent on everything that is stronger than itself.

Granted.

ἐστιν ἔχειν, ὅταν θέλῃς καὶ ἐφ' ὅσον θέλεις καὶ οἷον θέλεις ;—Οὔ.—Τὰ δὲ δουλάρια ;—Οὔ.—Τὰ δ' ἱμάτια ;—Οὔ.—Τὸ δὲ οἰκίδιον ;—Οὔ.—Τοὺς δ' ἵππους ;—Τούτων μὲν οὐδέν.—Ἂν δὲ τὰ τέκνα σου ζῆν θέλῃς ἐξ ἅπαντος ἢ τὴν γυναῖκα ἢ τὸν ἀδελφὸν ἢ τοὺς φίλους, ἐπὶ σοί ἐστιν ;—Οὐδὲ ταῦτα.

Πότερον οὖν οὐδὲν ἔχεις αὐτεξούσιον, ὃ ἐπὶ μόνῳ ἐστὶ σοί, ἢ ἔχεις τι τοιοῦτον;—Οὐκ οἶδα. —Ὅρα οὖν οὕτως καὶ σκέψαι αὐτό. μή τις δύναταί σε ποιῆσαι συγκαταθέσθαι τῷ ψεύδει ;

And is it up to you to have land whenever you want, for as long as you want, in the condition that you want?

It is not.

And likewise in the case of slaves, clothes, house, and horses?

None of these either.

And if more than anything you want your children to stay alive or your wife or your brother or your friends, are these things just up to you?

They are not.

Have you, then, nothing that is self-determined, that is up to yourself exclusively, or do you have such a thing?

I don't know.

Well, look at it like this and think about it. Can anyone make you assent to something untrue?

No one can.

—Οὐδείς.—Οὐκοῦν ἐν μὲν τῷ συγκαταθετικῷ τόπῳ ἀκώλυτος εἶ καὶ ἀνεμπόδιστος.—Ἔστω.—

Ἄγε, ὁρμῆσαι δέ σε ἐφ᾽ ὃ μὴ θέλεις τις δύναται ἀναγκάσαι ;—Δύναται. ὅταν γάρ μοι θάνατον ἢ δεσμὰ ἀπειλῇ, ἀναγκάζει μ᾽ ὁρμῆσαι.—Ἂν οὖν καταφρονῇς τοῦ ἀποθανεῖν καὶ τοῦ δεδέσθαι, ἔτι αὐτοῦ ἐπιστρέφῃ ;—Οὔ.—Σὸν οὖν ἐστιν ἔργον τὸ καταφρονεῖν θανάτου ἢ οὐ σόν ; —Ἐμόν.—Σὸν ἄρα ἐστὶ καὶ τὸ ὁρμῆσαι ἢ οὔ ;—Ἔστω ἐμόν.—Τὸ δ᾽ ἀφορμῆσαι τίνος ; σὸν καὶ τοῦτο.—

Therefore, in the domain of assent you are unimpeded and unconstrained.

Granted.

Let's continue: can someone compel you to have a motivation for something you do not want?

They can: whenever they threaten me with death or with fetters, they compel me to have such a motivation.

Suppose, though, that you disdain dying and being fettered; are you still going to pay attention to them?

I am not.

Is disdaining death your own function, then, or does it not belong to you?

It is mine.

So being motivated is also your own function, or is it not?

I grant that it is.

Τί οὖν, ἂν ἐμοῦ ὁρμήσαντος περιπατῆσαι
ἐκεῖνός με κωλύσῃ ;—Τί σου κωλύσει ; μή τι τὴν
συγκατάθεσιν ;—Οὔ· ἀλλὰ τὸ σωμάτιον.—Ναί,
ὡς λίθον.—Ἔστω· ἀλλ᾽ οὐκέτι ἐγὼ περιπατῶ.—

Τίς δέ σοι εἶπεν " τὸ περιπατῆσαι σὸν ἔργον
ἐστὶν ἀκώλυτον " ; ἐγὼ γὰρ ἐκεῖνο ἔλεγον
ἀκώλυτον μόνον τὸ ὁρμῆσαι· ὅπου δὲ σώματος
χρεία καὶ τῆς ἐκ τούτου συνεργείας, πάλαι
ἀκήκοας, ὅτι οὐδέν ἐστι σόν.—Ἔστω καὶ
ταῦτα.—Ὀρέγεσθαι δέ σε οὗ μὴ θέλεις τις
ἀναγκάσαι δύναται ;—Οὐδείς.—Προθέσθαι

And repulsion from something? That is also yours.

What if I am motivated to take a walk and another person impedes me.

What part of you will they impede? Surely not your assent?

No, but my poor body.

Yes, as they would impede a stone.

Let that be so, but the fact is that I don't continue with my walk.

And who told you, "It is your function to walk unimpeded"? What I have been telling you is that the only unimpeded thing is the motivation. Wherever there is a need for the body and the body's cooperation, you have heard long ago that none of it is your own.

I grant that as well.

Can anyone compel you to desire something that you don't want?

No one can.

δ' ἢ ἐπιβαλέσθαι τις ἢ ἁπλῶς χρῆσθαι ταῖς
προσπιπτούσαις φαντασίαις ;—Οὐδὲ τοῦτο· ἀλλὰ
ὀρεγόμενόν με κωλύσει τυχεῖν οὗ ὀρέγομαι.—Ἂν
τῶν σῶν τινὸς ὀρέγῃ καὶ τῶν ἀκωλύτων, πῶς σε
κωλύσει ;—Οὐδαμῶς.—Τίς οὖν σοι λέγει, ὅτι ὁ
τῶν ἀλλοτρίων ὀρεγόμενος ἀκώλυτός ἐστιν ;

Ὑγείας οὖν μὴ ὀρέγωμαι ;—Μηδαμῶς, μηδ'
ἄλλου ἀλλοτρίου μηδενός. ὃ γὰρ οὐκ ἔστιν ἐπὶ
σοὶ παρασκευάσαι ἢ τηρῆσαι ὅτε θέλεις, τοῦτο
ἀλλότριόν ἐστιν. μακρὰν ἀπ' αὐτοῦ οὐ μόνον τὰς
χεῖρας, ἀλλὰ πολὺ πρότερον τὴν ὄρεξιν· εἰ δὲ

Can anyone exert compulsion over your intentions and projects, or to speak quite generally, can anyone manipulate the way you deal with the impressions you experience?

Not that either; but when I do desire something, they will stop me from getting what I desire.

But how will they stop you if you desire one of the things that are your own and not liable to impediment?

In no way at all.

So who is telling you that you can be free from impediment if you desire things that are not your own?

Am I not to desire health, then?

Certainly not, and nothing else that is not your own, because nothing is your own that is not up to you to procure or to secure whenever you want. Keep your hands right off it, but first and foremost keep your desire well

μή, παρέδωκας σαυτὸν δοῦλον, ὑπέθηκας τὸν
τράχηλον, ὅ τι ἂν θαυμάσῃς τῶν μὴ σῶν, ᾧ τινι
ἂν τῶν ὑπευθύνων καὶ θνητῶν προσπαθῇς. —Ἡ
χεὶρ οὐκ ἔστιν ἐμή ;—Μέρος ἐστὶ σόν, φύσει δὲ
πηλός, κωλυτόν, ἀναγκαστόν, δοῦλον παντὸς τοῦ
ἰσχυροτέρου. καὶ τί σοι λέγω χεῖρα ; ὅλον τὸ σῶμα
οὕτως ἔχειν σε δεῖ ὡς ὀνάριον ἐπισεσαγμένον,
ἐφ᾽ ὅσον ἂν οἷόν τε ᾖ, ἐφ᾽ ὅσον ἂν διδῶται· ἂν δ᾽
ἀγγαρεία ᾖ καὶ στρατιώτης ἐπιλάβηται, ἄφες,
μὴ ἀντίτεινε μηδὲ γόγγυζε. εἰ δὲ μή, πληγὰς
λαβὼν οὐδὲν ἧττον ἀπολεῖς καὶ τὸ ὀνάριον. ὅταν
δὲ πρὸς τὸ σῶμα οὕτως ἔχειν σε δέῃ, ὅρα, τί
ἀπολείπεται περὶ τὰ ἄλλα, ὅσα τοῦ σώματος
ἕνεκα παρασκευάζεται. ὅταν ἐκεῖνο ὀνάριον ᾖ,
τἆλλα γίνεται χαλινάρια τοῦ ὀναρίου, σαγμάτια,
ὑποδημάτια, κριθαί, χόρτος. ἄφες κἀκεῖνα,
ἀπόλυε θᾶττον καὶ εὐκολώτερον ἢ τὸ ὀνάριον.

away. Otherwise, you are giving yourself up to slavery and submitting your neck to the yoke, if ever you admire what is not your own and feel strongly for things that are dependent on others and are perishable.

Isn't my hand my own?

It is a part of you, but by nature it is clay, subject to impediment and compulsion, a slave to everything that is stronger. And why do I mention your hand to you? You should treat your entire body like a little overloaded donkey, just as long as that is possible and allowed to you. But if it is pressed into public service and a soldier seizes it, let it go and don't resist or grumble. If you do, you will get a beating and lose your little donkey just the same. Since this is the attitude you need to have to the body, consider what you need to do about the rest of the things that one gets for the sake of the body. Since the body is a little donkey,

4.5.27–32

πάντα πανταχοῦ θνητά, εὐάλωτα, οἷς τισιν τὸν
ὁπωσοῦν προσέχοντα πᾶσα ἀνάγκη ταράσσεσθαι,
κακελπιστεῖν, φοβεῖσθαι, πενθεῖν, ἀτελεῖς
ἔχειν τὰς ὀρέξεις, περιπτωτικὰς ἔχειν τὰς
ἐκκλίσεις. εἶτα οὐ θέλομεν τὴν μόνην δεδομένην
ἡμῖν ἀσφάλειαν ἐχυρὰν ποιεῖν ; οὐδ᾽ ἀποστάντες
τῶν θνητῶν καὶ δούλων τὰ ἀθάνατα καὶ φύσει
ἐλεύθερα ἐκπονεῖν ; οὐδὲ μεμνήμεθα, ὅτι οὔτε
βλάπτει ἄλλος ἄλλον οὔτε ὠφελεῖ, ἀλλὰ τὸ περὶ
ἑκάστου τούτων δόγμα, τοῦτό ἐστι τὸ βλάπτον,
τοῦτο τὸ ἀνατρέπον, τοῦτο μάχη, τοῦτο στάσις,
τοῦτο πόλεμος ;

everything else becomes bridles, saddles, shoes, barley, and hay for the donkey. Let them go too. Dismiss them more quickly and more easily than the donkey itself.

5 Knowing What to Want

Everything everywhere is perishable and vulnerable. If you get attached to some of them even a little, you are bound to be troubled and discouraged, a prey to anxiety and distress. You will have desires that are unfulfilled and aversions that are fully realized. Are we not willing, therefore, to secure the only safety that has been granted to us—to give up the perishable and slavish things, and work on those that are imperishable and naturally free? Don't we recall that no one does injury or benefit to another, but that the cause of each of these things is a judgment. This is what does harm

FROM THE *DISCOURSES*

Ἐτεοκλέα καὶ Πολυνείκη τὸ πεποιηκὸς οὐκ ἄλλο ἢ τοῦτο, τὸ δόγμα τὸ περὶ τυραννίδος, τὸ δόγμα τὸ περὶ φυγῆς, ὅτι τὸ μὲν ἔσχατον τῶν κακῶν, τὸ δὲ μέγιστον τῶν ἀγαθῶν. φύσις δ' αὕτη παντός, τὸ διώκειν τὸ ἀγαθόν, φεύγειν τὸ κακόν· τὸν ἀφαιρούμενον θατέρου καὶ περιβάλλοντα τῷ ἐναντίῳ, τοῦτον ἡγεῖσθαι πολέμιον, ἐπίβουλον, κἂν ἀδελφὸς ᾖ, κἂν υἱός, κἂν πατήρ· τοῦ γὰρ ἀγαθοῦ συγγενέστερον οὐδέν. λοιπὸν εἰ ταῦτα ἀγαθὰ καὶ κακά, οὔτε πατὴρ υἱοῖς φίλος οὔτ' ἀδελφὸς ἀδελφῷ, πάντα δὲ πανταχοῦ μεστὰ πολεμίων, ἐπιβούλων, συκοφαντῶν. εἰ δ' οἷα δεῖ προαίρεσις, τοῦτο μόνον ἀγαθόν ἐστιν, καὶ οἷα μὴ δεῖ, τοῦτο μόνον κακόν, ποῦ ἔτι μάχη, ποῦ λοιδορία; περὶ τίνων; περὶ τῶν οὐδὲν πρὸς ἡμᾶς; πρὸς τίνας; πρὸς τοὺς ἀγνοοῦντας, πρὸς τοὺς δυστυχοῦντας, πρὸς τοὺς ἠπατημένους περὶ τῶν μεγίστων;

and wreckage, it is this that is battle, this that is strife, and this that is war.

What made *Eteocles and Polyneices the mortal foes that they were was simply this— their judgment concerning kingship and their judgment concerning exile. They judged the latter to be the worst of bad things and the former to be the greatest of goods. This is everyone's nature, to pursue the good and avoid the bad, and to regard a person who deprives us of the one and inflicts us with the other as an enemy and a schemer, even if he is a brother or a son or a father; for nothing is more closely related to us than the good.

So if these things are good and bad, no father is dear to his sons, and no brother is dear to his brother, but everything is full of enemies, plotters, and informers. But if the right will is the only good thing and the wrong will the only bad thing, what place is left for battle, what place for

1.17.21–28

Ἄνθρωπε, προαίρεσιν ἔχεις ἀκώλυτον φύσει καὶ
ἀνανάγκαστον . . .

δείξω σοι αὐτὸ πρῶτον ἐπὶ τοῦ συγκαταθετικοῦ
τόπου. μή τίς σε κωλῦσαι δύναται ἐπινεῦσαι
ἀληθεῖ; οὐδὲ εἷς. μή τίς σε ἀναγκάσαι δύναται
παραδέξασθαι τὸ ψεῦδος; οὐδὲ εἷς. ὁρᾷς ὅτι ἐν
τούτῳ τῷ τόπῳ τὸ προαιρετικὸν ἔχεις ἀκώλυτον
ἀνανάγκαστον ἀπαραπόδιστον; ἄγε ἐπὶ δὲ τοῦ
ὀρεκτικοῦ καὶ ὁρμητικοῦ ἄλλως ἔχει; καὶ τίς
ὁρμὴν νικῆσαι δύναται ἢ ἄλλη ὁρμή; τίς δ' ὄρεξιν
καὶ ἔκκλισιν ἢ ἄλλη ὄρεξις καὶ ἔκκλισις; "ἄν μοι,"

abuse? About what things? About things that are nothing to us? Against whom? Against the ignorant, against the unfortunate, against people who have been deceived about what matters most?

6 Freedom of the Will

Look, my friend, you have a will that is by nature unimpeded and unconstrained. . . . I will prove it you, first, in the area of assent. Can anyone prevent you from assenting to a truth?

No one can.

Can anyone compel you to accept a falsehood?

No one can.

Do you see that in this area you have a will that is unimpeded, unconstrained, unhindered? Come now, is it different in the area of desire and motivation? What can overcome a motivation except another motivation? What can overcome a desire or an aversion except another desire or aversion?

φησί, "προσάγῃ θανάτου φόβον, ἀναγκάζει με."
οὐ τὸ προσαγόμενον, ἀλλ' ὅτι δοκεῖ σοι κρεῖττον
εἶναι ποιῆσαί τι τούτων ἢ ἀποθανεῖν. πάλιν οὖν τὸ
σὸν δόγμα σε ἠνάγκασεν, τοῦτ' ἔστι προαίρεσιν
προαίρεσις. εἰ γὰρ τὸ ἴδιον μέρος, ὃ ἡμῖν ἔδωκεν
ἀποσπάσας ὁ θεός, ὑπ' αὐτοῦ ἢ ὑπ' ἄλλου τινὸς
κωλυτὸν ἢ ἀναγκαστὸν κατεσκευάκει, οὐκέτι ἂν
ἦν θεὸς οὐδ ἐπεμελεῖτο ἡμῶν ὃν δεῖ τρόπον. . . .
ἐὰν θέλῃς, ἐλεύθερος εἶ· ἐὰν θέλῃς, μέμψῃ οὐδένα,
ἐγκαλέσεις οὐδενί, πάντα κατὰ γνώμην ἔσται
ἅμα τὴν σὴν καὶ τὴν τοῦ θεοῦ.

1.6.12–21

Πολλὰ μὲν ἐπὶ μόνων, ὧν ἐξαιρέτως χρείαν εἶχεν
τὸ λογικὸν ζῷον, πολλὰ δὲ κοινὰ εὑρήσεις ἡμῖν

Yet if someone threatens me with the fear of death, they do compel me.

What compels you is not the threat but your decision that it is better to do something else rather than die. Once again, then, it is your judgment that compelled you; in other words, will compelled will. For if God, in taking from himself his own special part, which he has given to us, had constructed it to be impeded or constrained by himself or by something else, he would no longer be God or be caring for us as he should. If you so will it, you are free; if you so will it, you will blame no one, accuse no one, and everything will be in accord both with your own judgment and with God's.

7 Making Correct Use of Impressions

We are endowed with many attributes that are uniquely requisite for rational creatures, but, as

καὶ πρὸς τὰ ἄλογα. ἆρ᾽ οὖν καὶ παρακολουθεῖ
τοῖς γινομένοις ἐκεῖνα; οὐδαμῶς. ἄλλο γάρ
ἐστι χρῆσις καὶ ἄλλο παρακολούθησις. ἐκείνων
χρείαν εἶχεν ὁ θεὸς χρωμένων ταῖς φαντασίαις,
ἡμῶν δὲ παρακολουθούντων τῇ χρήσει. διὰ
τοῦτο ἐκείνοις μὲν ἀρκεῖ τὸ ἐσθίειν καὶ πίνειν
καὶ τὸ ἀναπαύεσθαι καὶ ὀχεύειν καὶ τἆλλ᾽ ὅσα
ἐπιτελεῖ τῶν αὐτῶν ἕκαστον, ἡμῖν δ᾽, οἷς καὶ τὴν
παρακολουθητικὴν δύναμιν ἔδωκεν, οὐκέτι ταῦτ᾽
ἀπαρκεῖ, ἀλλ᾽ ἂν μὴ κατὰ τρόπον καὶ τεταγμένως
καὶ ἀκολούθως τῇ ἑκάστου φύσει καὶ κατασκευῇ
πράττωμεν, οὐκέτι τοῦ τέλους τευξόμεθα τοῦ
ἑαυτῶν.

Ὧν γὰρ αἱ κατασκευαὶ διάφοροι, τούτων καὶ
τὰ ἔργα καὶ τὰ τέλη. οὗ τοίνυν ἡ κατασκευὴ

you will find, we also share many faculties with the animals that lack ability to reason.

Do they too pay attention to what happens?

By no means. "Using" and "paying attention" are quite different from one another. God needed the other animals as creatures that make use of their impressions, but he needed us as creatures who pay attention to how we use them. Therefore, it is sufficient for them to eat and drink and rest and copulate, and do everything else that each kind of animal does. For us, on the other hand, to whom God has also given the *power of paying attention, these animal activities are no longer sufficient, but unless we act appropriately and methodically and in harmony with our individual nature and constitution, we shall no longer attain our own ends.

Beings that have different constitutions also have different functions and ends. In those whose constitution is designed for use alone,

μόνον χρηστική, τούτῳ χρῆσθαι ὁπωσοῦν
ἀπαρκεῖ· οὗ δὲ καὶ παρακολουθητικὴ τῇ χρήσει,
τούτῳ τὸ κατὰ τρόπον ἂν μὴ προσῇ οὐδέποτε
τεύξεται τοῦ τέλους.

Τί οὖν;

Ἐκείνων ἕκαστον κατασκευάζει τὸ μὲν ὥστ᾽
ἐσθίεσθαι, τὸ δ᾽ ὥστε ὑπηρετεῖν εἰς γεωργίαν,
τὸ δ᾽ ὥστε τυρὸν φέρειν, τὸ δ᾽ ἄλλο ἐπ᾽ ἄλλῃ
χρείᾳ παραπλησίῳ, πρὸς ἃ τίς χρεία τοῦ
παρακολουθεῖν ταῖς φαντασίαις καὶ ταύτας
διακρίνειν δύνασθαι; τὸν δ᾽ ἄνθρωπον θεατὴν
εἰσήγαγεν αὐτοῦ τε καὶ τῶν ἔργων τῶν αὐτοῦ,
καὶ οὐ μόνον θεατήν, ἀλλὰ καὶ ἐξηγητὴν αὐτῶν.
διὰ τοῦτο αἰσχρόν ἐστι τῷ ἀνθρώπῳ ἄρχεσθαι καὶ
καταλήγειν ὅπου καὶ τὰ ἄλογα, ἀλλὰ μᾶλλον ἔνθεν
μὲν ἄρχεσθαι, καταλήγειν δὲ ἐφ᾽ ὃ κατέληξεν ἐφ᾽
ἡμῶν καὶ ἡ φύσις. κατέληξεν δ᾽ ἐπὶ θεωρίαν καὶ
παρακολούθησιν καὶ σύμφωνον διεξαγωγὴν τῇ
φύσει. ὁρᾶτε οὖν, μὴ ἀθέατοι τούτων ἀποθάνητε.

use of that constitution is quite sufficient. But those who have the additional power of paying attention will never attain their ends unless they exercise this faculty properly.

What, then, is the consequence?

God constituted each of the other animals, either to be eaten, or to serve in farming, or to produce cheese, or for some other comparable use. To perform these functions, what need do they have of the power to pay attention to impressions and to discriminate between them? But God introduced human beings to be students of himself and his works, and not merely students but also interpreters of these things. It is wrong, therefore, for us to begin and end where the nonrational animals do; we should rather begin where they do but end where nature has ended in our case. Nature ended at studying and paying attention to things and a way of life in harmony with itself. See to it,

4.7.7–17

Τὰ μὲν οὖν ἄλλα πάντα ἀπήλλακται τοῦ
δύνασθαι παρακολουθεῖν τῇ διοικήσει αὐτοῦ· τὸ
δὲ λογικὸν ζῷον ἀφορμὰς ἔχει πρὸς ἀναλογισμὸν
τούτων ἁπάντων, ὅτι τε μέρος ἐστὶ καὶ ποῖόν
τι μέρος καὶ ὅτι τὰ μέρη τοῖς ὅλοις εἴκειν ἔχει
καλῶς. πρὸς τούτοις δὲ φύσει γενναῖον καὶ
μεγαλόψυχον καὶ ἐλεύθερον γενόμενον ὁρᾷ,
διότι τῶν περὶ αὐτὸ τὰ μὲν ἀκώλυτα ἔχει καὶ ἐπ᾽
αὐτῷ, τὰ δὲ κωλυτὰ καὶ ἐπ᾽ ἄλλοις· ἀκώλυτα μὲν
τὰ προαιρετικά, κωλυτὰ δὲ τὰ ἀπροαίρετα. καὶ
διὰ τοῦτο, ἐὰν μὲν ἐν τούτοις μόνοις ἡγήσηται τὸ

then, that you do not die without having studied these things.

8 Freedom and Human Nature

All the other creatures have been left without the ability to pay attention to the world's divine government. Rational animals, however, have resources for reasoning about all these things, and to conclude that they themselves are a part of the world, a part of a particular kind, and also that it is right for the parts to give way to the whole. Furthermore, since it is their nature to be noble, high-minded, and free, they see that they are positioned in a world where some things are unimpeded and up to them, while other things are liable to impediment and up to others. Things of the first kind belong to the sphere of the will, while those that are outside it are liable to impediment. Accordingly, if rational animals restrict their own good and

ἀγαθὸν τὸ αὑτοῦ καὶ συμφέρον, τοῖς ἀκωλύτοις
καὶ ἐφ᾽ ἑαυτῷ, ἐλεύθερον ἔσται, εὔρουν,
εὔδαιμον, ἀβλαβές, μεγαλόφρον, εὐσεβές, χάριν
ἔχον ὑπὲρ πάντων τῷ θεῷ, μηδαμοῦ μεμφόμενον
μηδενὶ τῶν γενομένων, μηδενὶ ἐγκαλοῦν· ἂν δ᾽ ἐν
τοῖς ἐκτὸς καὶ ἀπροαιρέτοις, ἀνάγκη κωλύεσθαι
αὐτό, ἐμποδίζεσθαι, δουλεύειν τοῖς ἐκείνων
ἔχουσιν ἐξουσίαν, ἃ τεθαύμακεν καὶ φοβεῖται,
ἀνάγκη δ᾽ ἀσεβὲς εἶναι ἅτε βλάπτεσθαι οἰόμενον
ὑπὸ τοῦ θεοῦ καὶ ἄνισον, ἀεὶ αὑτῷ τοῦ πλείονος
περιποιητικόν, ἀνάγκη δὲ καὶ ταπεινὸν εἶναι καὶ
μικροπρεπές.

Ταῦτα τί κωλύει διαλαβόντα ζῆν κούφως
καὶ εὐηνίως, πάντα τὰ συμβαίνειν δυνάμενα
πράως ἐκδεχόμενον, τὰ δ᾽ ἤδη συμβεβηκότα

interest to the former kind alone—the things that are unimpeded and up to themselves—they will be free, contented, happy, unharmed, high-minded, reverent, grateful to God for all things, never finding fault with anything that has happened, or blaming anyone. If, on the other hand, they identity their good and interest with things that are external and outside the sphere of the will, they are bound to be impeded and frustrated, subservient to those who have authority over the things that they have admired and fear; they are also bound to be utterly irreverent, since they think that God has a grudge against them, and to be unfair, since they always grab more for themselves; and they are bound to lack self-respect and generosity.

If you understand these truths, what is to stop you from living in a free and easy way, calmly accepting everything that can happen and putting up with what has already taken

φέροντα ; " θέλεις πενίαν ; " φέρε καὶ γνώσῃ, τί
ἐστὶ πενία τυχοῦσα καλοῦ ὑποκριτοῦ. " θέλεις
ἀρχάς ; " φέρε. θέλεις ἀναρχίαν ; φέρε. ἀλλὰ
πόνους θέλεις ; φέρε καὶ πόνους. " ἀλλ᾽ ἐξορισμόν ; "
ὅπου ἂν ἀπέλθω, ἐκεῖ μοι καλῶς ἔσται· καὶ
γὰρ ἐνθάδε οὐ διὰ τὸν τόπον ἦν μοι καλῶς,
ἀλλὰ διὰ τὰ δόγματα, ἃ μέλλω μετ᾽ ἐμαυτοῦ
ἀποφέρειν. οὐδὲ γὰρ δύναταί τις ἀφελέσθαι
αὐτά, ἀλλὰ ταῦτα μόνα ἐμά ἐστι καὶ ἀναφαίρετα
καὶ ἀρκεῖ μοι παρόντα, ὅπου ἂν ὦ καὶ ὅ τι ἂν
ποιῶ. " ἀλλ᾽ ἤδη καιρὸς ἀποθανεῖν." τί λέγεις
ἀποθανεῖν ; μὴ τραγῴδει τὸ πρᾶγμα, ἀλλ᾽ εἰπὲ
ὡς ἔχει " ἤδη καιρὸς τὴν ὕλην, ἐξ ὧν συνῆλθεν,
εἰς ἐκεῖνα πάλιν ἀποκαταστῆναι." καὶ τί δεινόν ;
τί μέλλει ἀπόλλυσθαι τῶν ἐν τῷ κόσμῳ, τί
γενέσθαι καινόν, παράλογον ; τούτων ἕνεκα

place? "Do you want me to be poor?" Bring it on, and you will learn what poverty is when a good actor plays that part. "Do you want me to hold office?" Bring it on. "Do you want me to leave office?" Bring that on too. "Do you want me to endure pains?" Bring them on as well. "And exile?" Wherever I go, I will be fine, because I was already fine here—not on account of the place but as a result of my principles, and I am going to take them with me. No one can take them away from me; they are my only possessions, irremovable ones that are enough for me wherever I am and whatever I do.

"But it's now time for you to die."

Why do you say "to die"? Don't make it into a tragic business. Tell it as it is – "It's now time for the material you are made of to *return to the source it first came from." What's terrible about that? What is the world about to lose of its contents, what strange and unheard of thing

φοβερός ἐστιν ὁ τύραννος ; διὰ ταῦτα οἱ δορυφόροι
μεγάλας δοκοῦσιν ἔχειν τὰς μαχαίρας καὶ ὀξείας ;
ἄλλοις ταῦτα· ἐμοὶ δ' ἔσκπται περὶ πάντων, εἰς
ἐμὲ οὐδεὶς ἐξουσαν ἔχει. ἠλευθέρωμαι ὑπὸ τοῦ
θεοῦ, ἔγνωκα αὐτοῦ τὰς ἐντολάς, οὐκέτι οὐδεὶς
δουλαγωγῆσαί με δύναται, καρπιστὴν ἔχω οἷον
δεῖ, δικαστὰς οἵους δεῖ.

1.6.37–42

Ἀπόβλεψον εἰς τὰς δυνάμεις ἃς ἔχεις καὶ ἀπιδὼν
εἰπὲ "φέρε νῦν, ὦ Ζεῦ, ἣν θέλεις περίστασιν·
ἔχω γὰρ παρασκευὴν ἐκ σοῦ μοι δεδομένην καὶ
ἀφορμὰς πρὸς τὸ κοσμῆσαι διὰ τῶν ἀποβαινόντων
ἐμαυτόν." οὔ· ἀλλὰ κάθησθε τὰ μὲν μὴ συμβῇ
τρέμοντες, τῶν δὲ συμβαινόντων ὀδυρόμενοι
καὶ πενθοῦντες καὶ στένοντες· εἶτα τοῖς θεοῖς
ἐγκαλεῖτε. τί γάρ ἐστιν ἄλλο ἀκόλουθον τῇ
τοιαύτῃ ἀγεννείᾳ ἢ καὶ ἀσέβεια; καίτοι ὅ γε θεὸς

is going to happen? Is it for this that the tyrant makes us afraid? Is this why the swords of the guards seem long and sharp? Let others worry about that. Having looked into it all, I find that no one has authority over me. I have been liberated by God, I have gotten to know his commands, no one has power any longer to enslave me, I have the right kind of emancipator and the right kind of judges."

9 Freedom and Dignity

Study the powers that you have, and then say: "Bring on now, O Zeus, whatever circumstance you like; for I have the equipment and resources, bestowed on me by yourself, to distinguish myself by means of the things that come to pass." No! You sit trembling for fear of what may happen, weeping, wailing, and groaning over what actually is happening, and then you put the blame on the gods; for the feebleness

οὐ μόνον ἔδωκεν ἡμῖν τὰς δυνάμεις ταύτας, καθ᾽
ἃς οἴσομεν πᾶν τὸ ἀποβαῖνον μὴ ταπεινούμενοι
μηδὲ συγκλώμενοι ὑπ᾽ αὐτοῦ, ἀλλ᾽ ὃ ἦν ἀγαθοῦ
βασιλέως καὶ ταῖς ἀληθείαις πατρός, ἀκώλυτον
τοῦτο ἔδωκεν, ἀνανάγκαστον, ἀπαραπόδιστον,
ὅλον αὐτὸ ἐφ᾽ ἡμῖν ἐποίησεν οὐδ᾽ αὐτῷ τινα
πρὸς τοῦτο ἰσχὺν ἀπολιπών, ὥστε κωλῦσαι ἢ
ἐμποδίσαι. ταῦτα ἔχοντες ἐλεύθερα καὶ ὑμέτερα
μὴ χρῆσθε αὐτοῖς μηδ᾽ αἰσθάνεσθε τίνα εἰλήφατε
καὶ παρὰ τίνος, ἀλλὰ κάθησθε πενθοῦντες καὶ
στένοντες.

that you display amounts to nothing short of impiety. Yet God has not only given us these powers as the means for us to bear everything that happens without being humiliated and crushed by them, he has also, like a good king and a true father, given them without impediment or constraint or hindrance. He has made them entirely up to us, without reserving even for himself any power to impede or hinder. Since you have these powers free and entirely your own, why don't you put them to use and take cognizance of what gifts you have received and from what donor you have received them instead of sitting grief-stricken and groaning?

ACKNOWLEDGMENTS

The instigation to write this book came to me from Rob Tempio of Princeton University Press. He envisioned it as an appropriate addition to the press's "Ancient Guide" series, and he has been with me all the way by giving encouragement and advice. I am most grateful to him, and to Matt Rohal, Sara Lerner, and Jay Boggis, who shepherded the book through its production with great care and skill. I warmly thank Brad Inwood and Monique Elias, who read and improved my first go at translating the *Encheiridion*. Andrea Nightingale read an earlier draft of the introduction, and responded to it with her characteristic skill and generosity. The anonymous readers consulted by the press also suggested points that have improved the work. I also want to remember Rob Dobbin,

ACKNOWLEDGMENTS

who passed away while this book was being copyedited. Rob, who was one of my first graduate students at Berkeley, made outstanding contributions to the study of Epictetus. I frequently consulted his books as I was writing this work.

To David Sedley, wonderful friend and collaborator, I dedicate the book with great affection and admiration.

GLOSSARY

ANTECEDENTS and CONSEQUENCES Epictetus draws on the terminology Stoic logicians used for expressing the rule of inference called *modus ponens*, signifying "If this, then that."

APPROPRIATE ACTIONS Technical term (Greek *kathēkonta*) for the behavior that conforms in general to the specific nature of living things. It covers both self-interested actions such as avoiding danger to oneself, and other-regarding behavior such as caring for offspring and community.

ASSENT Technical term (Greek *synkatathesis*) for the mental faculty that constitutes a person's capacity to approve or disapprove the truth and value of impressions, and issue corresponding motivations or impulses. In Stoic sources (e.g., Cicero, *De fato*) assent is called the "principal cause" of human action and the locus of agency and autonomy; see p. xliv.

ATTENTION, POWER OF PAYING Technical term (Greek *parakolouthēsis*) for the distinctively human ability to monitor and interpret impressions.

AVERSION Technical term (Greek *ekklisis*) for a strongly negative attitude toward what appears bad.

BAD In Stoicism, "bad" (*kakos*) applies only to what is morally at fault, meaning a flawed character and dishonorable action. The world as such, in its own nature, contains nothing bad.

CAPTAIN Metaphor for the Stoics' providential divinity.

CHRYSIPPUS Third head of the Stoic school at Athens (third century BC) and its most authoritative and voluminous writer.

COMMANDING-FACULTY Technical term (Greek *hēgemonikon*) for the mind or principal part of the human soul, consisting in reason, whose function is to govern the self and authorize its behavior.

CONJUNCTIVE and DISJUNCTIVE STATEMENT Axioms of Stoic logic. In *Encheiridion* 36,

Epictetus mentions them in order to play on the Greek word *axia*, meaning both logical validity and human value.

DESIRE Technical term (Greek *orexis*) for a strong acquisitive attitude toward what appears good.

DIG ALONGSIDE The athletic activity envisioned by this word (Greek *parorussesthai*), supplied from the almost verbatim *Discourse* 3.15, is obscure. From the details that follow, Epictetus seems to envision a bout of wrestling in a pit dug up by the contestants.

DIOGENES (fl. mid fourth century BC) founder of Cynic philosophy and one of Epictetus's iconic figures.

DONOR Metaphor for the Stoics' providential divinity.

EMBRACING STATUES Epictetus deprecates the Cynics' practice of nakedly embracing statues in cold weather as a way of displaying hardiness.

ENDORSEMENT See assent.

ETEOCLES and POLYNEICES The sons of Oedipus who had been cursed by him to kill one another and later quarreled over succession to their father's throne; see p. 131.

EUPHRATES (late first-century AD) a Stoic philosopher renowned for his lecturing skill. He is mentioned twice by Epictetus in the *Discourses*, and editors generally supply his name here as a correction to the MSS that write the more familiar name Socrates.

FREEDOM Epictetus's Greek word *eleutheria* covers freedom quite generally. The primary sense of *libertas*, its Latin equivalent, was the status of a free person as distinct from that of a slave. Epictetus constantly plays on this ambiguity, treating Stoic philosophy as if it were manumission from actual slavery, and actual freedom, when untrained in Stoic philosophy, as enslavement to passions and false beliefs.

GOD(s) Used in the singular, or by the name of Zeus, to designate the world's providential creator and omnipresent agent, equivalent to nature, fate, and cosmic reason (*logos*), embodied in fiery breath (*pneuma*), and present to human beings in their rational faculty. Used in the plural as a concession to popular polytheism, whereby gods name such features of nature as sun (Apollo) and ocean (Poseidon) or mind (Athena) and reason (Hermes).

GOOD In Stoicism "good" (*agathos* in Greek) applies only to what is "honorable" (*kalon* in Greek), meaning a virtuous character and virtuous action.

HARMONY OF THE UNIVERSE Harmony (Greek *symphonia*) invokes the Stoics' favorite musical model for a unitary structure. The unity of opposites is an idea that looks back to the early Greek philosophers Pythagoras and Heraclitus.

HARMONY WITH NATURE Technical phrase for the Stoic's goal—to behave in conformity both to one's human nature as a rational animal and to one's predetermined and god-given circumstances.

HERACLES Mythical strong man and slayer of monsters, appropriated as a philosophical model by Cynics and Stoics. The manuscripts of Epictetus write the name Heraclitus at this point, but I follow Louis-André Dorion in thinking that this name should be emended to Heracles.

GLOSSARY

IMPRESSION Technical term (Greek *phantasia*), sometimes translated by "appearance," for whatever is immediately present to the mind, either as a sense experience or as a thought. Epictetus likes to describe the Stoic project as learning how to "use" and "interpret" impressions correctly; see p. 137.

INDIFFERENT Technical term (Greek *adiaphoros*) for things that are neither good nor bad, taken by themselves, but are susceptible to good or bad use by those who experience them.

INDUBITABLE IMPRESSIONS Technical phrase (*phantasiai katalēptikai*) for sense experiences or thoughts that self-evidently represent things as they truly are.

MOTIVATION Technical term, often translated by "impulse" (Greek *hormē*), for the mental faculty that prompts performance of actions, and depends on assent to impressions.

NATURAL AFFINITY Technical term (Greek *oikeiōsis*) for the self-preservative and social instincts of living creatures, which serve as the naturalistic foundation of ethics in Stoicism.

NATURE'S PURPOSE The phrase signifies things that are bound to happen, given the circumstances, and irrespective of their effects on the individuals involved.

OBOL Small silver coin.

PEOPLE OUTSIDE YOUR CIRCLE The Greek expression (*idiōtai*) covers "ordinary people," as I translate it in other passages of the *Encheiridion*, but Epictetus also uses it to mark off nonphilosophers.

PRAETOR A high-ranking position in Roman civil service and provincial administration.

PRODUCER Metaphor for the Stoics' providential divinity.

PROGRESS Technical term (Greek *prokopē*) for persons who have committed themselves to Stoicism as their philosophy of life and who make every effort to improve their performance.

PUBLIC LECTURES It was common practice at the time of Epictetus for poets, philosophers, and orators to exhibit their work in public readings.

PYTHIAN APOLLO Epictetus refers to the god Apollo in his function as source of the oracles delivered at his Delphic shrine. The point of the anecdote is that you don't need an oracle to decide whether to go to the assistance of a friend in danger.

QUOTATIONS The four quoted passages are (1) four verses by the Stoic philosopher Cleanthes, (2), two verses from a lost play by the tragedian Euripides, and (3–4) statements Plato assigns to Socrates in *Crito* 43d and *Apology* 30c.

RESERVATION A technical term (Greek *hypexairesis*) for the way rational agents should qualify or "hold back" their inclinations and disinclinations, in order to adjust them to the future's uncertainty.

RETURN Epictetus uses the Stoics' technical term for the world's eventual absorption of all its elements and their reconstitution and recurrence in an everlasting and identical cycle.

ROLE This word (Greek *prosōpon*, meaning theatrical part or person) is Epictetus's favorite term to express the individual identity or character people reveal in the way they perform their familial and social positions.

GLOSSARY

SATURNALIA The name of the annual December festival at which Roman slaves were given a day of total freedom with license to insult their masters and be waited on at table.

SOCRATES (470–399 BC) Athenian philosopher, executed on charges of impiety and corrupting the young, and treated by Epictetus as the ideal human being. In *Enchiridion* 32 Epictetus alludes to an anecdote reported by Xenophon in his *Memoirs of Socrates* 1,1,7, and in 46 he seems to refer to the beginning of Plato's dialogue *Protagoras*.

THINGS CONTRARY TO NATURE Technical phrase (Greek *ta para physin*) for anything in Stoicism that conflicts with optimal human well-being. The expression often refers to such conditions as bodily sickness and poverty, which we are naturally motivated to try to avoid. Because successful avoidance of such things is not simply "up to us," Epictetus restricts the scope of the term here to aberrant mental states. He takes these states (e.g., pathological emotions and unethical motivations) to be contrary to the rational norms of human nature, entirely "up to us," and therefore fully avoidable.

TRANQUILITY The ideal Stoic mentality, expressed here by two catch words of Hellenistic philosophy *apatheia* (literally "being unaffected") and *ataraxia* (literally "being undisturbed").

WILL A favorite term in Epictetus (Greek *prohairesis*) for a human being's power of self-determination and mental disposition. The word is sometimes translated by choice, purpose, volition, or decision, but in my opinion "will" is the most natural English expression for what Epictetus seeks to convey with it.

ZENO Refers to the Cypriot founder of the Stoic school at Athens in about 300 BC.

FURTHER READING

Greek Editions of the *Discourses*

Boter, G. *The Encheiridion of Epictetus and Its Three Christian Adaptations*. Leiden: Brill, 1999.

Schenkl, H. *Dissertationes ab Arriano Digestae*. Leipzig: Teubner, 1916.

Complete Translations of Epictetus

Hard, R. *Epictetus: Discourses, Fragments, Handbook*. Oxford: Oxford University, Press, 2014.

Oldfather, W. A. *Epictetus*. 2 vols. including Greek text. Cambridge, Mass.: Harvard University Press, 1925–1928.

Translations of the *Encheiridion*

Boter, G. *The Encheiridion of Epictetus and Its Three Christian Adaptations*. Leiden: Brill, 1999.

Dobbin, R. *Epictetus, Discourses and Selected Writings*. New York: Penguin, 2008.

Gourinat, J.-B. *Premières leçons sur le Manuel d'Epictète*. Paris: Presses Universitaires de France, 1998.

Hard, R. in C. Gill, ed. *The Discourses of Epictetus*. Rutland, Vt.: Everyman, 1993.

Higginson T. W. *Epictetus, The Enchiridion*. Upper Saddle River, N.J.: Library of Liberal Arts, 1948.

Long, G. *Enchiridion*. Amherst, N.Y.: Prometheus Books, 1991; repr. of nineteenth–century translation.

Oldfather, W. A. *Epictetus*. Vol. 2. Cambridge, Mass.: Harvard University Press, 1928.

White, N. P. Epictetus, *The Handbook*. Indianapolis, Ind.: Hackett, 1983.

Studies of Stoicism and Epictetus

Brandt, U. *Kommentar zu Epiktets Encheiridion*. Heidelberg: Universitätsverlag Winter, 2015.

Brennan, T., and C. Brittain. *Simplicius on Epictetus' "Handbook 27–53."* 2 vols. Ithaca, N.Y.: Cornell University Press, 2002.

Brennan, T. *The Stoic Life: Emotions, Duties, Fate.* Oxford: Clarendon Press, 2005.

FURTHER READING

Dobbin, R. Epictetus *Discourses Book I.* Oxford: Clarendon Press, 1998.

Frede, M. A. *Free Will: Origins of the Notion in Ancient Thought.* Berkeley: University of California Press, 2011.

Graver, M. R. *Stoicism and Emotion.* Chicago: University of Chicago Press, 2007.

Inwood, B. *Ethics and Human Action in Early Stoicism.* Oxford: Clarendon Press, 1985.

Johnson, B. E. *The Role Ethics of Epictetus: Stoicism in Ordinary Life.* Lanham, Md.: Rowman & Littlefield, 2014.

Long, A. A. *Hellenistic Philosophy: Stoics, Epicureans, Sceptics.* 2nd ed. Berkeley: University of California Press, 1986.

———. *Stoic Studies.* Berkeley: University of California Press, 1996.

———. *Epictetus: A Stoic and Socratic Guide to Life.* Oxford: Clarendon Press, 2002.

———. *From Epicurus to Epictetus.* Oxford: Clarendon Press, 2006.

Sellars, J. *Stoicism.* Berkeley: University of California Press, 2006.

Sorabji, R. *Emotion and Peace of Mind: From Stoic Agitation to Christian Temptation.* Oxford: Oxford University Press, 2000.

Stephens, W. A. *Stoic Ethics: Epictetus. Happiness as Freedom.* London: Continuum, 2007.

Studies of Freedom

Berlin, I. "Two Concepts of Liberty." In M. Sandel, ed., *Liberalism and Its Critics.* New York: New York University Press, 1984, 15–36.

Patterson, O. *Freedom in the Making of Western Culture.* New York: Harper Collins, 1991.

INDEX

INDEX

INDEX

INDEX

INDEX